You Have the Power...

You Have The Power...

Vanessa J. Jones, J.D.

AND

Theresa R. Joseph

Ivy Press

Mississippi

Ivy Press
P.O. Box 1554
Hattiesburg, MS 39403-1554

Copyright © 2001 by Vanessa J. Jones and Theresa R. Joseph.
All rights reserved.
including the right of reproduction
in whole or in part in any form.

Ivy Press Edition 2001

Manufactured in the United States of America

Library of Congress Cataloging-in-Publication Data

Jones, Vanessa J., 1969-
You have the power— / Vanessa J. Jones and Theresa R. Joseph.
p. cm.
Includes index.
ISBN 0-9709356-0-9 (pbk. : alk. paper)
1. Women—Psychology. 2. Women—Life skills guides. 3. African American women—Psychology. 4. African American women—Life skills guides. 5. Self-realization. I. Joseph, Theresa R., 1969- II. Title.
HQ1206 .J65 2001
646.7'0082—dc21
2001001428

CONTENTS

ACKNOWLEDGMENTS ix

INTRODUCTIONS xiii

SECTION ONE: INOCULATE YOURSELF
WITH THE "I LOVE ME" VACCINE 1

1. Understand the Woman/Child in the Mirror 3
2. Know From Where Thine Cometh 9
3. Be a Role Model for Your Child 13
4. Education Builds Confidence 17

SECTION TWO: THE PROFESSIONAL 25

5. Separate the Personal From the Professional 27
6. Promote Yourself, Be Your Own Portfolio
   & Resume, Blow Your Own Horn 49

SECTION THREE: ROMANCE 55

7. What Are You Looking for in a Man
(Where Are You Looking)? 57

8. What Has He Done for You Lately (Today)? 63

9. Compromise is the Key. 69

10. How Will a Man Help You Attain Your Goals? 73

11. Love Builds Relationships,
Respect Sustains Marriages. 77

12. Stroke Your Man's Ego 89

SECTION FOUR: THE FINANCIAL 93

13. Girl, You Need to Handle Your Business. 95

14. Insure Your Family's Future 105

15. My Will Be Done 109

SECTION FIVE: THE PERSONAL............115

16. If You Don't Take Care of You,
Who Will Care for Your Children?...............117

17. Health Issues Women Face..................121

18. Set Aside Me Time........................125

19. I am Responsible for My Own Happiness.......129

AFTERWORD...............................135

NOTES....................................137

INDEX....................................139

ACKNOWLEDGMENTS

A special thanks to Gloria Shropshire and Elijah Jones for their editing jobs. You helped this book come to life! Also to Jimmie Jones, thanks for the initial editing. You helped put our disjointed words into the beginnings of a book. To all our other family and friends, Kenneth B. Johnson, Linda Ferdinand, Michele Howard, and Yvette thanks for your support and words of encouragement.

This book is dedicated to our families

To my husband, Bill, thanks for being my refuge.
You encouraged and motivated me to write when I didn't believe in myself.
To my two little rascals, Trey and Miles, Mommy loves you.
Bertha, Harvey, Maria, John, Kenny, and Ennis, thanks for always being there for me.

Vanessa J. Jones

To the God sent love of my life who always understands me,
even in times of extreme madness, my heart and soul,
Kenneth Joseph.
To the best family in the entire world,
Bueford, Jean, and Eileen Spain.

Theresa R. Joseph

Introduction by Vanessa

I often wondered why was I repeating the same mistakes over and over again in my personal life, as well as professional life. I would actively seek the path of self-destruction when the straight and narrow were easier to follow. Everything kept going back to my childhood. Looking in the mirror as an adult, I still saw a child who still felt unloved. In order to be complete, I knew I had to find my inner strength to deal with the inner demons of that child in the mirror.

You Have the Power..... highlights, through personal experiences and anecdotes, how to tap into your inner strength, to deal with issues and situations so you can turn your life around, and find your power to live a successful life. We share our journey and how we obtained that power. In this book, you will discover that "You Have The Power!"

Introduction by Theresa

The writing of this book was a therapeutic process for Vanessa and I. We went through life with blinders on singing, "Oh Woe is Me," until we realized that other people were experiencing the same pain, dissolution, and insecurities as we were. We hope that the women reading this book, whether you are African-American, Caucasian, Asian, Native American, Hispanic or Latino, will realize that the experiences we talk about and try to resolve, although they may have a "sister girl" slant to them, are not just "black issues." They are issues that are universal to women.

This book is designed to be a guide to empower women, and to serve as a road map to help others avoid the pitfalls that hindered my journey to greatness. Moreover, it will show you that you are not alone, and that where you came from does not have to be your final destination in life.

Ladies, we hope to educate and entertain. But in the end, we hope that this work will help you to grow. We are not saying that you won't ever have troubles or strife. However, take a chapter from our drama filled lives. You are a rose about to flower. Lovely, lovely ladies, *You Will Have the Power*.

SECTION ONE:

INOCULATE YOURSELF WITH THE "I LOVE ME" VACCINE

Chapter One

Understand the Woman/Child in the Mirror

Little child what do you know?
My little child how will you grow?
Am I giving you all the love that you need?
Am I giving you all the tools to succeed?
When I was a child, I had to find my own way;
When I was a child, I had no time to play.
I did my best to hide from the world
And when I look in the mirror,
I still see that frightened little girl.
Little child the world will be better for you;
I promise to give you the tools to make it through.
I will nurture your spirit, your body, and your soul;
You will succeed; you will achieve your life's goal.

During the Christmas holidays of the year 2000, my family and I were sitting at home channel surfing and caught an entertainer being interviewed on television. Bear in mind, I was not a fan of the artist and often wondered what all the hype was about. As far as I was concerned, she would not know how to reach an octave if you gave her a ladder! My hand paused on the remote as we listened to what she had to say. She talked about coming of age in an inner-city project and how despite her millions of dollars, notoriety, and fame, she still suffered from low self-esteem. She internalized her problems by drowning her sorrows in a bottle rather than facing them. She sought comfort in food rather than putting herself up for rejection from those she loved. She accepted sex instead of love, because she questioned whether or not she deserved love. Suddenly, I realized that it was not necessarily her voice, but the message of her music and shared experiences that served as hope for a forgotten group of people in the inner cities of America.

Most of us had childhood insecurities, whether it was weight, lack of confidence or acne that made us feel like such an ugly duckling. As adults, you have to face these insecurities head on. Otherwise, every time you look in the mirror, you see that fat, unloved child, no matter how thin you are. No matter how clear a complexion you have, you still see that invisible zit. No matter how articulate you are, you still see a stuttering child with no self-confidence.

As a child, I remembered family members would say, "Shut up with your big lips." I started perching my lips to make them look smaller and thinner. All the models on television had thin lips and were tall and thin with long hair.

They set the standard for what America perceived as beautiful. I had none of those attributes and I thought I was the ugliest child alive.

When I was a teenager I recall a situation of my cousin preparing for her wedding. This was a cousin that I had idolized since she had come to live with us (while her parents "worked things out"). She was thin, with long hair, and beautiful. I was dark, with short hair, and pleasantly plump. I loved her with all the love of a sister. It came to pass that she was to marry her childhood sweetheart, when she was only seventeen. While at her house working on the wedding, and unaware that I had entered the house, I overheard someone ask her if I was going to be in her wedding. "Oh, no!" was her reply, "I don't want any fat people in my wedding?" Needless to say, my little twelve-year-old heart was crushed. I eased out, and never said a word, but someone else told my mother. None of us attended the wedding. The episode had a profound, and almost deadly effect on me. I became obsessed with being thin, almost to the point of Anorexia. And why? So I could fit into someone else's opinion of what was beautiful.

I started on various diets to obtain a model's figure. This one diet promised that you would loose ten pounds in three days. You had to eat a hot dog, a boiled egg, and a banana three time a day. It fell short of its promise. At the end of the diet, I would be weak to the point of passing out. I probably lost about three pounds, but for a teenager every pound counted. I couldn't wait to regain my strength, to see if the next time I could loose five instead of three pounds.

As if the weight wasn't enough to deal with, I also had

a severe case of acne. I couldn't stand to look at myself in the mirror and no matter how hard I scrubbed and washed, the bumps kept coming. Every month, I grew a huge pimple in the most conspicuous place on my face. I could feel it growing inside my skin. It would start to pulsate as it struggled to "pop" to the skin surface. I would scream, "Oh God, not again." I knew that in a day or two, my little friend would be making his appearance. Most of the time, one would "pop up" right on the tip of my nose.

Once during my senior year of high school, I was walking down the hall between classes. I heard someone say, "Did you see that bump on her nose?" Both students began to laugh uncontrollably. I wanted to crawl into the nearest corner and die. When I took my senior portrait, my little friend sat right on the tip of my nose. I can imagine it was saying, "Girlfriend, how dare you try to hide me on such a special occasion." I finally had to admit to myself, that acne was a problem that I had to learn to live with. It was going to flare up every now and then. I wouldn't have skin like a run way model. Thank God that as we get older, we get smarter and learn that beauty is in the eye of the beholder, and you are the beholder.

No matter how successful you are, you have to deal with the inner demons of your childhood in order to truly be happy. You can have the world in the palm of your hands, as that entertainer did, but unless you understand your childhood, it's hard to accept success. From that, you actively seek the path of self destruction, although, you know the straight and narrow-path is easier to follow. You wonder, "Why am I repeating the same mistakes over and over again?" The reason you do this is because the inner child is screaming for love, yet she has not learned to love herself. If you don't learn to love yourself, you will allow people to do and say despicable things to you. You have the tendency to believe them, because you have not inoculated yourself with the "I Love Me Vaccine." You have to love yourself, no matter what packaging the body comes in. Whether you're big, tall, fat, or skinny, reach deep into your inner self and find your power to say, "To heck with what society says. I am beautiful." Remember, no one can make you feel inferior unless you give them the power to.

You deserve love, and so does your inner child. Innoculate yourself with the "I Love Me" vaccine. Once inoculated with this vaccine, none of the nasty diseases such as negativity, spitefulness, self-doubt, jealousy, or vindictiveness can get a strong enough hold to do you any permanent damage. Sure, you will come down with a case of the self-doubt every now and then. However, once your "I Love Me" antibodies start to multiply, self doubt would soon be conquered. *You Will Have The Power!*

Chapter Two

Know From Where Thine Cometh

"History, despite its wrenching pain, cannot be unlived, and if faced with courage, need not be lived again." Maya Angelou, Inaugural Poem, 20 January 1993

Coming from a small town in Mississippi, we were poor. We cornered the market on the ghetto canapes. The butter, sugar, and mayonnaise sandwiches. We were recycling long before it became the politically correct thing to do! One tub of water could wash at least two children.

My mother had her first child at fifteen, her second at sixteen, and by the time she was twenty, she had four children by two different fathers. The Johnson household was a madhouse. You could hear drunken laughter intermixed with the sounds of Z.Z. Hill singing "Down Home Blues" all weekend long. These activities often led to loud arguments and fights. I remember my mother and stepfather in physical confrontations. My mother would end up with a bloody nose. The next thing I knew I would hear grunts of pleasure coming from the bedroom. Grownups were like Martians to me. No matter how hard I tried, I couldn't understand their behavior.

Early in life, I learned the importance of setting priorities. Weekends were a time for play. They should not interfere with the work week. Like clock work, on Monday mornings, order was restored to the household. My mother rose early for work. The children likewise had to rise to attend school and our report cards were monitored to ensure that we were passing. She did not ask that we make A's and B's. Passing was acceptable in our house. She knew education would give us power to succeed in life.

A railroad track divided our neighborhood into poor and poorer sections. At the age of six, my family moved from the poorer to the poor side of the track. After we moved, my mother told me not to go back across the track and hang out with my friends. After she told me that, I thought to myself, "Who is she to tell me who to hang out with?" At the time, I did not understand that this change in my environment was necessary to put me on the road to success and to break the cycle of mediocrity. I didn't realize that you are who you hang around. So, when she left home, I went across the tracks anyway. I thought, "She would never know." Little did I know that Ms. Bean, our elderly neighbor, watched my every move from her front porch. Today, we have the neighborhood watch. Back in those days, we had an "Old-folk watch." I could pass her house twenty times a day. Every time I passed, I had to acknowledge her presence. If I didn't, she would tell my mother, "Vanessa was being sassy today." I had to give her that good ol' southern respect.

Every time I went across the tracks, Ms. Bean would tell and I would get a whipping. This battle of wills between my mother and I lasted about six months. Eventually, my mother won. I waved my white flag and surrendered to her will. She knew what it would take to get her daughter on the path to greatness. *She Had The Power.*

Acting White

When I was seven, my mother enrolled my brother, Kenny, and I in a summer integration program. Poor black children from Mississippi spent summers with white families in Wisconsin. I spent the summer of 1975 with the Smiths in Sun Prairie, Wisconsin. When I visited, the Smith household was wild and chaotic. Molly was a divorced mother with four children. Two weeks prior to my scheduled visit, Molly and her family were involved in a car accident. It was raining and Molly lost control of the car. Her youngest daughter, Stormy, was critically injured and in a coma. A week into my visit, she died.

I saw three black faces the entire time I was there. Every time we went to the market, I was the star attraction. It was a scary feeling standing out in the crowd. I resented my mother for shipping me off to live with white people. Who was she to try and broaden my horizons? Who did she think she was?

After my visit to Wisconsin, I was teased about the way I talked. Family members would say, "She's acting white." I remember my great-grandmother saying, "Where did she get that talk from." Criticisms like these made me a shy and introverted person. In my seven-year-old mind, I thought that if I did not say anything, I would not be singled out to be ridiculed. I wanted to scream and tell everyone that I was the same little girl they always knew, "My Momma sent me off to live with white people; how could I not pick up some of their mannerisms?" I thank God for helping me understand that family members and friends sometimes have a cruel way of loving you.

However, little did I know that this experience would have a life long affect on me. It helped shape me into the confident woman that I am today. I learned during the three summers that I spent with the Smiths that white people eat, breathe, hurt, and cry just like we do. They are no better or smarter than you are. When you get down to the basics we are all the same and our ultimate goal in life is to find happiness. No matter what anyone says, God put me here to make a difference. I will not disappoint him. I will speak, walk, and talk like the lady that I am. I will display my Power.

Today, our household would be labeled dysfunctional. But, you know what? Somehow it worked. All five of us have high school diplomas. Two of us have college degrees. Two are career military. That's not bad for a single mother from Oxberry, Mississippi. She instilled the power in us!

Chapter Three

Be a Role Model for Your Child

Our children are our most precious natural resource. Unlike plants and trees, they do not get their nutrition from the air. They may not listen to what we say all of the time, but they are going to emulate our actions every time! Spend time (if only an hour a night) with your children. Young children learn how to be adults by watching and mimicking the role models around them. The same goes for how they learn professionalism and work ethics. The inner ingredients for success do not miraculously happen overnight. The evolution of success begins the moment a child is born. Our families, neighborhoods, and churches play an important part in our developing into productive citizens.

Place importance on education early in your children's lives. Be an active participant in your children's education. Stimulate your children's minds. Expand their knowledge and expose them to the arts. Share the joys of reading with them. The greatest gift a friend gave to me in the seventh grade was a book. She opened my eyes to the world of reading. Reading was my escape from everyday household problems. I always kept my nose buried in a good book. To get my undivided attention, family members would hide the book I was reading. I would travel all over the world and back, vicariously that is, through the characters in Danielle Steele's novels. I even envisioned myself writing one day. My stories would be an inspiration for little girls to rise above their circumstances. I would give them the Power.

In today's society, most parents are working outside the home to make ends meet. More than likely, they are spending less time with their children. Most of their day is spent at work. Children do not understand that parents have to work to pay the bills. And frankly, they really don't care. All they know is the job seems to be more important to my mom and dad than I am. But if you don't take time to teach them how to be independent, the gangs will. Exercise power over your child's future.

Talk to your children about the mistakes you made and let them know that mistakes happen and that they have to learn from them. Talk to them also about what you did to become the success that you are. It will give them more confidence. The road to success may not be as difficult for them as it was for you. Let them know that although it is good to have other people's opinions, the only opinions that count are theirs and the people that love them.

A child's confidence and inner tranquility come when she learns to love herself. Her self-esteem needs to be nurtured starting in infancy. When she loves herself, she won't settle for less than the best. When you promote a child's self-esteem, you cut out the middleman. She will not believe others when they try to belittle her or her accomplishments.

Make your children self-sufficient and confident. It is the confident children that can stand up against peer pressure. They will make smart decisions and will lead the pack instead of lagging behind. Anyone can follow. Following requires very little effort. Teach your children to be leaders. Your children will be able to jump over any obstacle that they find in their path. They will have the power.

Chapter Four

Education Builds Confidence

Without knowledge, you would be ignorant of the vast opportunities to succeed in this world. Everyone has the right to receive an education in any educational facility he or she chooses. To define, receiving education is the ability to learn from one who is qualified to teach and to take that knowledge, reprocess it to suit your goals, and set out to accomplish those goals. Once this occurs, confidence is sure to surface, because achievement has been conquered.

With that, educational facilities have been established with an array of options to fit a person's needs based on his career choice or what that school has to offer him. For example, some may wonder what happens to those individuals who have difficulty adjusting to a higher learning institution, because of their low scores in basic reading, writing, and arithmetic. From that, I am aware that there are community colleges and historically black colleges and universities providing such services for these students.

A lot of people ask, "Do Historically Black Colleges and Universities (HBCUs) serve a purpose in today's society?" My answer to them is, "Yes." They serve a vital purpose for young adults who haven't acquired basic reading, writing, and math skills in high school or those that need a more nurturing environment. Most of these students don't have a shot of being accepted into Ivy League schools. As long as there is a disparity in educational access for disadvantaged students, HBCUs are needed.

Have you ever watched, "Who Wants to be a Millionaire?" It shows the vast differences in male/female and black/white educations in America. I've seen fewer than ten black contestants on the show. I am not counting the celebrity editions. Very few of them make it to the hot seat. The questions "Millionaire" ask are geared for middle class white males. Consequently, have you noticed when asked the easiest question about African-Americans, the contestants usually have to use a "Life Line?"

While in high school, my English teacher, who was prepping us for a test, told our class, "If you are black, the verb you think is right is probably wrong." You learn to speak from listening to your parents. How is it that everything you learn is wrong? To be competitive, some students have to unlearn what they have learned at home. It's amazing. This teacher taught a lot of things in her class. The one thing that stood out in my sixteen-year-old mind was this statement that she made. Be careful what you say around children. It's little things like this that they remember and that have a lasting impact on their lives.

In August of 1987, I started my freshman year at Alcorn State University. Theresa and I lived on the same floor in the freshman dorm. I was a Political Science major. She was a Sociology major. During our junior year, we became close friends while in the Reserve Officers Training Corps (R.O.T.C.).

Captain Ashton, one of the R.O.T.C. cadre members, was well traveled, tall, fine, and educated. We liked to say, "He had it going on." He felt that it was his duty to educate us "poor southern hicks." Every Monday, Wednesday, and Friday at 6:00 a.m., we ran P.T. (physical training). Running the hills of Alcorn with my big behind was no easy task. I was thick back then. As the saying goes, I had some "meat on my bones." I remember Captain A, our nickname for him, screaming, "Ms. Johnson, you're going to have to use it or lose it. Meaning basically, you have to work with what you have. If what you have is holding you back, you need to get rid of it, then and only then will you have the power to succeed!

After joining R.O.T.C., I was promoted from a private to a cadet, which is an officer in training, in my army national guard unit. It was the big talk of the unit whether they were going to give me the vacant cadet slot. I traveled all over the state to get a slot, because, my unit did not want to give me one of theirs. Finally to keep their numbers, they gave me the slot.

I will never forget how I was treated. I was the first black female to travel the officer ranks in my unit. The officers were supposed to train and guide me. However, I was never invited to any of the training meetings. Instead, they ignored me and acted like I didn't exist.

At my last summer training in 1991, a friend of mine overheard a senior officer say, "I hate the sight of her. I will be glad when she leaves." This was my first education and indoctrination that the world was not a fair place. These officers saw me as a threat. At the time, I was uneducated. I said to myself, "You just wait until I acquire more knowledge. You haven't seen anything yet." After that experience, I vowed to be better, do more and learn all that I could. I would have the Power.

You Must Burn The Midnight Oil

Dr. John Turner was my favorite college professor. He was a no nonsense kind of professor. He was six foot three, intelligent, and had a deep commanding voice which struck the fear of God in me. He told us about the real life experiences of Emmitt Till, Fannie Lou Hammer, Medgar Evers, and other civil rights leaders. I was amazed to hear their stories. In high school, I had never heard their names. He told us that as a result of being black, we were going to encounter many obstacles. But, we could not use obstacles as an excuse to rest on our laurels. We had to jump each hurdle and make life's twists and turns work for us. It was okay to fall, but we had to dust ourselves off and keep on trying.

He advocated education as a means of dealing with the curve balls that life was sure to throw our way. He was very quick to let us know that we were not special. He was not preaching negativity, but rather educating us on how the "real world" would view us and our "Historical Black College" education. You see, this was long before Tenesse Titan Quarterback, Steve McNair, a.k.a. "Air McNair" put Alcorn State University on the national radar, making the school a household name.

Dr. Turner taught by using the Socratic Method. Basically, he asked the questions and we answered them. We sat in our chairs praying that he would not call our name. He was not a professor you could fool into believing that you had read the assignment when you knew you hadn't. One day he said, "Ms. Johnson, brief *Brown vs. Board of Education*." I thought to myself, "I am going to get slammed dunked today." I stumbled through the case. His response to my performance was, "I see you called words last night." This was his way of saying you read the material, but you didn't comprehend a thing. I took six classes under Dr. Turner. I didn't receive an "A" until I took his last class. I stayed up many nights preparing for his class. Students had to burn the midnight oil to excel in his class.

Until You Learn to Communicate Effectively, You Will Always be a B-

History professor Dr. Kenroy Wilkians was another pillar and advocate for us "poor African-American children." He was no joke. He meant business. You learned one way or the other and he saw to it, personally. My biggest challenge was writing. Getting my thoughts down on paper was not the problem. It was hard to make my writing legible and readable. You see, I thought faster than I wrote. In order to get it all out before I forgot, I wrote fast. I was good at getting the info down, but, it was hard on the eyes. I thank God for typewriters back then, and computers today.

I will never forget the Monday morning back in 1989, I rushed to my eight o'clock class. On Friday, I turned in a "masterpiece" to Dr. Wilkians. Being as dramatic as ever, he made us sweat through the class before we knew our fate. I wasn't worried, no not me. At the end of the class, he began to pass out papers and he placed mine face down on the desk. To savor my victory, I left it face down. As everyone started to filter out, I turned the paper over. I could not believe he gave me a B-. I exclaimed, "Oh no, this was an A+ paper." I approached Dr. Wilkians to find out what was going on, with his back turned to me, he said, "Yes, Ms. Spain, what is it now?" We had a few similar conversations earlier in the semester. I said, "Dr. Wilkians, you gave me a B-. This is an 'A' paper." He replied, "I am sure it is, Ms. Spain. If I could have read more of it, you probably would have gotten an 'A'. The portion I could decipher deserved a B-." I got the picture. From then on, my papers were either printed, or typed on whoever's typewriter I could beg, borrow or steal. Dr. Wilkians taught me that no matter how smart I felt I was and that was quite smart, close to genius if you want to know the truth, that the world did not think I was anything special. Until I could effectively get my point across, I would always be a B-.

Sociology professor Dr. Alta (the be all and end all) Moran was a force to be reckoned with. Dr. Moran was in her early fifties. Our R.O.T.C. formation would pass her jogging at six a.m. After her morning jog, she would be waiting in her eight a.m. class at seven fifty when we began to straggle in. I was also fortunate, (uh huh, right), enough to have her for a three p.m. class. Whereas I would be showing signs of fatigue, she would be as bright-eyed and articulate as she was at eight a.m. Dr. Moran was the epitome of excellence and she demanded it from us as well.

I remember after one extremely long party. I missed her eight a.m. class. I had the audacity to show up for her three p.m. class. "Ms. Spain," she said, in her perfectly enunciated and articulated English, "I am happy to see you this afternoon, but I think you also had an eight a.m. appointment with me. I was there. Where were you?" I hunched in my chair and prayed for the floor to open up. She had pity on me and said, "I will be in my office at five p.m., and so will you." I got the picture; never again did I miss a class with Dr. Moran. Today, when I want to slack off and not give 100 percent, I can still see her looking down over her glasses at me with that, "I am not pleased and you will pay later" look on her face. Somehow, I find the motivation to complete my task. With the assistance of the aforementioned professors, I was able to develop the confidence in myself and in the education from the University. I earned the Power!

Where Was My Trust Fund

It takes a strong mind to rise above your beginnings. Why do some succeed who come from the same environment while others fall prey? Years after graduation from high school, you can go back to the neighborhood. Most of your childhood friends still live there. They are doing economically at about the same level as their parents. Some are doing worse. How are cycles of poverty broken? What are the keys to success?

After graduating from high school, one of my girlfriends decided to opt out of college and go straight into the workforce. She wanted to make a quick buck. If you want to achieve something, you have to sacrifice. Unless your grandparents left you a trust fund, there will be many days you will be flat broke. It took me seven grueling years of school. I lived on a financial roller coaster. I received student loans in August and January. If I spent all of my money, nothing was forthcoming. I learned to exercise power over my finances.

My first year out of law school, I made a lot more money than she made working two jobs. With each passing year, the gap in our income has widened. Recently, I was talking on the phone to this same friend. She was thinking about going to nursing school. I encouraged her to go ahead and do it. A couple of months later, she started having second thoughts. She said she would have to quit her job once she started the clinical portion of the nursing program. I told her nothing in life and worth having is easy. You have to set your priorities and work for what you want. Completing nursing school would have doubled her salary. Education would have given her the power to change her financial situation.

Theresa and I are two women from small towns in Mississippi. We worked hard and sacrificed to succeed in life. We took different paths along the way, but the final result was the same. Hard work and perseverance paid off. You too have the power to achieve anything you set your mind to. Education builds character, endurance, and patience. Why else would you pay thousands of dollars to listen to professors complicate formulas and theories? It is the best investment you can make. The return is bigger than any other stock market investment. It has financial and spiritual rewards that cannot be acquired elsewhere. Education is definitely the key to opening the doors of success. *It will give you the power!*

SECTION TWO
THE PROFESSIONAL

Chapter Five

Separate the Personal From the Professional

You call me on the weekend saying you have a problem
Could I Please help you out?
I've been there before, so I say surely,
What is it all about?
I listen very closely and then offer you advice;
You heave a sigh, try it out, and once again life is nice.

Well, bright and early Monday morning
I ask you to type a letter.
You roll your eyes, and give me the look that says,
"I know you know better."

Later in the week, I happen to ask you to do another task;
You turn your head and say something to your girls,
Then they begin to laugh.

What happened to my friend of last week?
That so badly needed me?
What about all the advice I have been giving you
Oh, by the way, for free.
What is this attitude that you can't seem to shake?
How much longer will we remain friends and you remain employed?
How much do you think I will take?

Vanessa went off to her career in law. I entered the army as a Second Lieutenant in the Military Police Corps. I figured the economy was bad (yes, at that age I was economy conscious). I will join, get some experience, maybe do four years and get out. However, Uncle Sam had other plans for me. I ended up staying twice as long, and doing things that I never thought I would do (jumping out of airplanes for instance). I do not regret my experiences for they were extremely educational and instrumental in making me the confident, splendid woman that I am today. Hey, once you've jumped out of an airplane at 3,500 feet, the rest is easy.

Well, I was advised prior to reaching my first duty station that my Battalion Sergeant Major, and my Company First Sergeant were serious racists. I thought about it for a while. Then, I came up with a plan. I scheduled an appointment on each of their calendars. I had the following conversation with each of them. "You know, I hear there is a lot of racism in this unit. Well you know what, each of us has our own prejudices. However, I think we should keep those feelings to ourselves, or until we are around other people that feel the same, and not let it interfere with our professional working relationships, what do you think?" Of course, they both agreed wholeheartedly. What else could they do? After that conversation, they both took extremely good care of me. You see they realized I was saying, "I know you are prejudice, and I am not trying to change your views. Just keep that personal, and don't let it interfere with the professional and everything will be fine." They did. Thank God!

While in the military, I heard my fellow lieutenants talk about how this one or that one is a "suck up" saying, "He is always in the boss' office." "He is always in his face." "Can he breathe?" I used to snicker at this language. Then, I saw life for those people was always so much better than mine. They were the ones getting the outstanding jobs. They were the ones getting the outstanding performance appraisals. They were the ones getting the good parking space.

I did not grasp the concept until I became a company commander. I hate golf. "Golf was the devil!" I thought. However, my boss was a golfer. He set golf dates, and made them optional, so I chose not go. But I started to realize that my fellow captains who went golfing with him had a better relationship with the boss. They had easy access to him and his time. I had to take the leftovers. What I'd failed to realize was that there were a lot of deals taking place on the golf course that I had no knowledge of. My boss' thing was golf. So guess what? I learned to play golf.

The military is not the only place where this works. It works everywhere. In today's society, being successful is also about "who you know," not just what you know. I know that I entered my present position on merit. However, it did not hurt that my sorority sister gave me the information, and the inside track on what points I should stress at the interview (the Ivy network at its best). Her help earned me a raise and a position of greater responsibility.

Who do you know? What professional organizations do you belong to? If your answer is none, it is not too late. What is your profession? I am sure it has a professional organization you can join. Do you have a degree? Is there a graduate chapter of a sorority you would like to join? Members can use your help in doing their good works. You can use the contacts that being a member brings with it. Vanessa and I are both partial to the "Pink and Green," Alpha Kappa Alpha Sorority, Inc.

The point is, it is not sucking up. It is coming up. It is not gaining favoritism. It is gaining ground. Your resume may be the best, but so are the others. What is the spark that will make them pick you? Who do you know? Who has the power?

Skills of Successful Women

*Ability to Separate the Personal from the Professional

Use emotion as your secret weapon. Oprah Winfrey's compassion has helped her become a very wealthy woman. Compassion is her trademark. People complain that she is always getting emotional on the air, always crying, but she cries all the way to the bank.

There is a stigma that women cannot work together. Women can work together. You have to separate the personal from the professional business. Women get caught up in emotions, but you have to understand that conflict happens in the *workplace*. It's not personal. It's office business.

Money changes behavior. Be up front. Explain your goals and expectations, because the team needs to be on the same sheet of music. If you are not, scream, shout, do whatever it takes for you to vent, just keep it behind closed doors. Then you move on and get down to the business of making money. It will give your business the power.

If your boss asks you to do something you don't want to do, be professional and do it anyway. Keep the attitude and neck swerving until you are alone. Most women have not reached the point that they are willing to take orders from another of their own sex. One is afraid that the other may prosper more than she does and be recognized accordingly. They don't realize that if they remain loyal and supportive, their friend's prosperity can become their own. You can ride your friend's coattails all the way to the bank. It's called mentor-ship.

Carter G. Woodson wrote in *The Mis-Education of the Negro* of an incident where a government department head hired an intelligent woman to supervise a group of women who were employed to do unskilled labor. Those working under her refused to obey instructions and kept the place in turmoil. Soon, they destroyed the morale of the whole force. Imagine that. Unfortunately, this is the same situation women find themselves in today. Hello. It's the twenty-first century. It is beyond time that we started taking as good care of each other in the work place as we do in the play place. If you can take a woman's advice about your man and what to do about him on the weekend, you should be able to take her advice on how the job needs to be done during the week day.

*Surround yourself with positive people

Successful people surround themselves with like minds. You should have common goals and ideals with the people with whom you associate. Now hold on! We are not saying you need to "sell out." What we are saying is that if the people around you are not helping you to inoculate yourself with the "I love me" vaccine, they may be contributing to the negativity disease.

For example, some athletes make it out of the inner city projects and enter the glamorous multimillionaire life. Time and time again they get caught up in the cycle of negativity, violence, and drug use. They have a hard time breaking their bond with the neighborhood. Just as I continued to go to the other side of the tracks, they continued to hang around people that were not working toward their professional or personal development. It took me a few whippings to understand this concept. Unfortunately, it is causing some promising young athletes their lives. How many times have we seen, heard, or read about some professional athlete being arrested, suspended, on trial, or dying? Where were they when these things happened to them? Who were they with? Was there a great deal of positivism going on? It's doubtful.

We are not trying to tell you that once you "make it" that you cannot maintain the friends that you had before. What we are saying is look at the lives these friends are leading. If they came from a bad neighborhood or if they have made bad decisions in life, what are they doing to improve their situation? If they are uneducated, are they returning to school (most communities offer GED classes)? If their attitudes are not correct, are they reading books to rectify it? If their emotions are a mess, are they seeking counseling? Are they a positive influence in your life? Can you learn from their examples? If the answer to the above questions is no, are they truly your friends?

A friend is someone who has your best interest at heart. He is a positive influence in your life. He wants you to succeed. He motivates you in a positive direction. If you get better, it is not threatening to him, but an accomplishment, because he helped you get there. Positivity nurtures power.

*Set realistic goals

You have to sit down and plot a chart of where you want your life to go. You need a one, five, and ten year plan. Your actions should be geared toward achieving these goals. Do not get discouraged if you have to change your goals to meet your current lifestyle. Your ultimate plan should be to reach or to get as close as possible to your ideal model of life.

You see, until our goals are written down, they are just abstract imaginations of our cerebral cortex. In other words, they are dreams. The process does not start until it is in writing. When you write something down, it becomes real, tangible, and attainable. First we dream; we plan; then, we get started towards making our own dreams a reality.

*Establish a good work ethic (If you're not going to do it, Just say no)
The meeting starts at nine but that means I don't have to really be there till nine ten

Oh, why is everybody looking at me when I enter

(Late, yet again)

I've worked here for years stuck in a position

that bores me to tears

Girl, do you want to go to lunch downtown to

meet that fine dude

Yes, I know we might be late getting back

(what's a few minutes one way or the other?)

> The boss calls me in, and I think finally
>   some recognition
>
> However, he tells me how the company is
>
> downsizing my position
>
> I'm fired, how dare they, 24/7 I gave them my best
>
> (Minus the times, I was late, more or less)

If you're supposed to be at work at 8:00 a.m., you need to be there. The truth is you need to be there at 7:50. Arriving at 8:15 is not acceptable. How much energy does it take to get up fifteen minutes earlier so you can get to work on time? Being late is not acceptable in corporate America.

Your word should be your bond. If you say that you are going to do something, *do it*. People are known for telling you that they are going to do something but then are either late or don't show up at all. You don't even get a courtesy call advising you that they are not going to show up. The next time you see them, they act like nothing happened and dare you to confront them about it. This may have been the norm in high school or college, but such triflingness should stop at adulthood and certainly once you become a professional.

Maggie started a new job. She was used to being late for everything. She continued her practice on her new job. She would arrive at work at eight-twenty a.m. She would leave for lunch at twelve and return at one-fifteen. Her day would end at four-fifty. How could she make a good impression on a new boss with these work habits?

Her office manager came into her office one day and slammed the door closed. She proceeded to say, "Our office opens at eight a.m. We close for lunch from twelve to one. Our day ends at five p.m. Do you think you can adhere to these rules?" Maggie looked up at her and rolled her eyes, as only a woman can, and replied, "Yes." What else can you say when you're caught in the wrong? Not a thing.

My co-workers are constantly surprised when I conduct training sessions that I can communicate effectively. They enjoy it and say, "nobody ever made me understand it that well before." My boss is still surprised that I am always ten minutes early to every meeting. The powers that be noticed my work ethics. As I type, I have been offered an executive level promotion with a house, and a raise.

*Know when to cut your losses, then move on

If you are in a dead-end job, move on. If you are in a dead end relationship, move on. If you have a dead-end friend, move on. If things are not working, do not continue to waste your time. Cut your losses and then, guess what? Move on.

I had a relationship that I truly regret. The relationship, like a weak battery on a car, continued to make me stall. I was no longer his "princess." I was his convenience. He was no longer my man. He was a demand. However, I stayed in the relationship out of comfort. In the meantime, I gained thirty pounds and almost lost all of my hair from stressing out over him. I was a mess.

Why, then, did I stay? Well I felt I had invested too much time and energy to "throw" the relationship away. But I didn't realize I was throwing away my youth, my health and my self-esteem by staying. Many of us have been guilty of the above behavior. But, guess what? It is time to shed the guilt and MOVE ON.

Likewise, you have to get out of your comfort zone if you want to succeed in the career world. I got a call from my personnel manager saying, "Have I got a position for you. The Old Guard is looking for a female platoon leader, and a female officer, with your outstanding record, you would be perfect." I asked him if I could call him back with my answer. I then looked up the Old Guard, a unit of great distinction that guards the tomb of the Unknown Soldier.

There had never been a female in the unit from its inception. This would be a great deal of pressure. I would constantly be under scrutiny at the national level. OH NO! I called him back and declined. I gave up an opportunity to be the "first," and the fame and glory that went with it.

When the news and magazine articles came out profiling the new female platoon leader, and what her background was (nothing as spectacular as mine), I felt envious. It could have been me. I could have been the "first," but I was stuck in my comfort zone.

Fast forward six years, and once again I am being offered the opportunity to be the "first" African-American female to hold a position. However, it entails moving to Oregon (where I will be the only African-American on staff, and one of two in town). It will entail my breaking outside of my comfort zone for it was an Executive (the corporate machine) leadership position. Did I take it, did I break out of my comfort zone? You bet I did! I realized my power.

Five Lessons of Success

*Success may not be received by others. Everybody will not be happy for you. Keep getting bigger and badder.

*You will become what you see yourself becoming.

*Reality is not what stops success, but giant fears.

*If you never see yourself successful, you will never be.

• Write it down, study, and become.

Attitude is Everything

> *"Ninety percent of the friction of daily life is caused by the wrong tone of voice."*

Good Morning, How are you?

What a lovely smile.

If there is anything you need, just ask.

I will be in the area for a while.

Good Afternoon, glad you came.

Do you know everyone here?

We are all long time friends.

It's so good to have you here.

Good evening, we want to welcome you.

We are so glad that you chose to come.

We've been searching for that special person,

And you are the perfect one.

Hello, who are you?

Where did you come from?

Someone will help you in a minute.

Sit there and fill out these forms.

Yes, may I help you?

You have an appointment with whom?

I'll buzz to see if they are ready or not.

I think you got here too soon.

What, you are who?

And what do you want with me?

Well, you will just have to sit and wait.

I'm on break until three.

If someone greeted you with any of the first phrases of the poem upon entering an interview, I am sure that you would feel an overwhelming sense of welcome. All of your anxiety, nervousness, and tension would leave your body. You would feel as if you had made the right decision to visit or relocate. However, if you received the salutations from the second scenarios, I don't think you would be too happy. In fact, I think you would become quiet attitudinal. Who do they think they are? Why should you wait? I already have a job, goodbye. Yeah, that seems about right.

The point is that in the personal and professional world, attitude is everything. I don't care if you are PMSing, having a bad hair day, having looked in your closet and even finding your fat clothes were tight, or dealing with a traffic mess. Once you arrive at work, you need to leave it at the curb.

For example, I took a new position. My plane got in late the night before. I checked into the hotel where I encountered a disgruntled employee on the desk. I got there at 2:30 a.m. and my room was not ready. Throughout the night, he routed wrong calls to my room. The next morning he did not give me my wake up call. I was almost late checking out. I was jet lagged when personnel from the job came to pick me up. However, I greeted them with a smile. I was not supposed to go into the office that day, but, there was a graduation going on and they wanted me to see it (Oh, what joy).

I was cranky, hungry, and wiped out. The last thing I wanted to do was to meet a whole lot of people. However, I pasted on a smile, flipped the switch to the good attitude, and soared through the day. They loved me. I used the Power!

Yes, it would have been easy to give in to my attitude, but to what avail? What would have been their impression of me? What message would I have sent about how I handle stress? What message would I have sent about female executives? Yes, what *one* of us does can and does affect *all* of us.

As a result of the move, none of my furniture was with me. However, that night a co-worker brought over a microwave, another brought a futon, another a mini refrigerator, and another a table and chair. I was fully furnished and able to wait until my goods got here. Was this because I was such a loveable person? No, but because I showed them a sunny personality and a good attitude. They recognized my Power.

Preparing for a Job Interview

It isn't fair that you worked for ten years and have loads of experience and several degrees and your fate is decided one way or the other in a 15 minute interview. Or should I say a five minute interview. Most interviewers know within the first five minutes you are in the room if they want to call you back for a second interview, hire you, or placate you until they can get you out of their office. (Don't call us, we'll call you.) So let me ask, what are you doing to prepare for an interview? How much time are you spending practicing? How much research have you done? I know some of you are saying, "Preparation, research, practice, what does that have to do with anything?" Look, not many of us would go and take a final exam without taking notes, studying, and then quizzing ourselves on the material. Well, think of your resume as the test, the telephone call (screening call) to set up the session as your midterm, and the interview as your final exam.

You need to do to these things to prepare. Every time you change positions you should update your resume. Ensure you have the most current copy on hand. Know your resume verbatim so that when you fill out the application it is the same information that you originally submitted (discrepancies could be intrepeted as lies).

When searching for a job, always answer the phone in a cordial manner. You never know if the next call is the one to set up an interview, or the screening call. If you answer with an attitude, what is their first impression of you? You won't get the job. Once the interview is set up, research the company. Find out the history, what your chain of command will be, what's important to the company right now. Once you have all of the information, practice saying it in the mirror. It is always nice when the interviewer asks "What do you know about the company?" and you have an accurate, articulate response.

Certain questions are generally asked at all interviews. What skills do you possess that qualify you for this position? Why should I hire you over the other applicants? What are your strengths? What are your weaknesses? Where do you see yourself in 5/10 years? What assets will you bring to this organization? Do you have any questions? You should think about, formulate, and write down your answers to these questions and become comfortable with your response.

The night before an interview you need to get a full night's rest. Get up and eat a nutritious meal. Leave home at least 45 minutes prior to your interview. Number one, traffic is always worse on the day of an interview. Number two, there are always forms to fill out. Number three, arriving early gives you a chance to get the layout of the land and get over some of your anxiety. It also gives a good first impression.

When you enter the room, smile, introduce yourself, and give a firm handshake. Compliment the interviewer on something (dress, shoes, a family photo, office). It puts him at ease and into a positive frame of mind. After this, take a deep breath to release your nervous tension and answer the questions with your articulate practiced responses.

If you follow these steps, the interviewer will be impressed and you will be a success. After the interview, be sure to send a "thank you for your consideration and time" card. It can only help. If you get called back for a second interview, repeat the preparation phase. The boss likes you and has narrowed the choices. You have the qualifications. Now, it is strictly personality and attitude that will get you the job. Let yours shine! If you don't get called for a second interview or hired, don't take it personally. There are other jobs out there. The more you practice, the better you will become. You are on the road to success and power.

**Find Out What You Enjoy Doing,
Become the Expert, and then
Find a Way to Make Money Doing It**

What is it that you are passionate about? Do you know how to make anything? What do you do better than anyone else in the world? Once you have figured this out, find out if there is a market for your skill or item? If not, decide if you want to take the time to develop a market. Remember. Someone has to be the first.

Once you have your market, find out how you want to advertise and to what audience. Start small. Your family members make great guinea pigs. (Ask our families how many times they had to read our manuscript before this book was published.) Most important, stick with it. If this commodity is your passion, you will do well. Eventually you will make it a success. Successful women are identifying the public's business need and filling it. They know that the most lucrative investment they can undertake is an investment in themselves. *The secret to a successful business is to find out what you enjoy doing, become the expert, and then find out how to make money doing it, thus this book.*

The original diva of hair care products, Madam C.J. Walker, endured a life of racism, sexism, and poverty. She was orphaned at seven, married at fourteen, and widowed by twenty-one. Those trials and tribulations did not stop her from becoming the nation's first self-made female millionaire. Madam Walker once stated, "I am a woman who came from the cotton fields of the South. I was promoted from there to the washtub. Then I was promoted to cook in the kitchen. And from there, I promoted myself into the business of manufacturing hair goods and preparations. Everybody told me I was making a mistake by going into this business, but I know how to grow hair as well as I know how to grow cotton." Madam Walker not only obtained great wealth, but she made entrepreneurship among hundreds of women possible. When you acquire wealth and knowledge, you should be a mentor to the young women who follow you.

Terrie Williams wrote in her book *Personal Touch* about an experience she had with a woman during her early years at *Essence* magazine. She placed a call to this woman in their sales department to request a copy of her media sales kit. The information requested was not top secret. Yet, this woman flatly refused to help her, for no reason. Well, four years later "Miss Thing" had the nerve to call and ask for a favor. She was interviewing for a job with the president of Essence, and she wanted advice and information on how best to handle him.

So, what do you think Terrie Williams did? What would you have done? Well, surprisingly, Terrie didn't hold a grudge. She did the right thing and answered her questions, prepared a package for her, and made sure she got everything she requested.

Terrie used the opportunity to remind her of the importance of being there for each another. She told her, "I would be remiss if I didn't remind you that a few short years ago, I asked you for some information and you flatly refused my request. Please let this be a life's lesson..... We all have to be there for one another. Knowledge is the platform for success and should be shared throughout the generations. Knowledge is power.

Each generation of successful women leaves fewer excuses for your not soaring to the top of your chosen profession. Each success story provides role models. Each success offers much needed encouragement for young teenagers and fills them with "I can do it to" vision. Success keeps those "I love me" inoculations flowing.

When I started practicing law, I made a point to offer excellent legal services whether it was a major liability suit, or welfare mothers' trying to receive child support. I treated everyone with dignity and respect. My partner and I interviewed several young women for our secretary/receptionist position. We decided to give a young, single mother a chance.

We told her, "You don't quite have the skills we are looking for, but we are willing to take a chance on you." Like a diamond in the rough, we felt that we could work with her and bring her out.

I explained to her that we were there to serve our customers and no matter how she felt, she needed to be nice to them. She was given a six-month probationary period to show some improvement. She finished her probationary period without a problem. Then, she started missing days. We explained to her that we had a three-person office. The absence of one puts a strain on the others. With an attitude, she told us, "I am only here to get some experience." Little did she know, she needed a good reference to go along with her experience. She could not see the big picture. She had an opportunity to do a good job and move onto bigger and better things when she got her degree. However, she did not take advantage of the opportunity we were providing. As a result, she ended up out of a job, out of a recommendation, and out of luck.

Each One, Teach One

Young girls learn how to be women by watching and mimicking the role models around them. The same goes for how they learn professionalism and work ethics. I was very fortunate (although, I didn't appreciate it at the time) to grow up in a household with a dual professional woman. My mother was a teacher and a minister. She has since received her PHD and is a principal.

At age eighteen, like so many young women, even though I watched her closely and gleaned her mannerisms, I did not appreciate what my mother had to offer. You know mothers can't tell their eighteen-year-old daughters anything. If my mother said it's black, I would say it's white, just to be trifling. It is only now, later in my life, that I realize what a jewel Dr. Bueford O. Spain is. At her knee, I learned how special I am. From her, I learned although the work week is Monday through Friday, we, women, must sometimes work on Saturdays to ensure that all "I's" are dotted and "T's" crossed. It was from her that I learned if you help others without any expectation, people notice and will treat and reward you accordingly. It was from her I learned dreams never die. If you continued to aspire to be great, eventually, you would have the power. That's what I learned and achieved.

Recently, I had to use my power. I was on a plane bound to Oregon. I struggled to put one bag in the overhead compartment. I realized that something I needed was in my second carry on. So, in order to not disturb the other passengers boarding, I moved into a row of empty seats so that I could dig freely. "Where is your seat?" was the snide question I heard in my ear? "I am in the seat behind these," I replied, "I am just getting out papers before I put this bag up." "I don't think so," this woman replied. " I don't think so either," was her husband's reply as he stuffed a bag above my head. "You are already taking up two spaces in that overhead," she snottily replied. " Who were these rude people? They did not know me, or how I would react to their rudeness?

I looked and saw a child eagerly listening to our conversation. I could have gone straight "sister girl." However, I asked the lady one simple question. "Is it necessary that you have an attitude and be rude?" As I looked into her eyes, she lowered her eyes. She looked away and said "No." I proceeded to get in my seat and placed the second bag under the seat (her seat in front of me).

My seat mate, an older lady asked, "Are you all right." I replied, "Yes, I am fine. I just don't see the need to be rude. What kind of example did that set for the children watching us?" She said so they could hear, "I agree. There is no reason to be rude. You handled that well." You see, somehow, in the heat of battle, I managed to exercise power over my emotions. Try it. You can, too.

Chapter Six

Promote Yourself, Be Your Own Portfolio and Resume, Blow Your Own Horn

"When I make my grand entrance into a crowded place
I try to greet everyone with a smile on my face
But, there is always someone who won't smile back
because, they're too busy trying to make a wise crack
about a single little strand of hair that might be out of place
or a spot of make-up that might show on my face
But, these kinds of people don't make me feel weak
I keep right on strutting and turn the other cheek.........

I'm proud of what I have to show
I walk with pride and let my qualities glow
Know some of us walk around with our

heads all up in the air
While those who envy us are always there to stare
It's not that we think we are the best in the crowd
It's just that we show our self appreciation straight forward
    and out loud
I'm amazed that I can stand on my own two feet
and not be ashamed around the people I meet
I know that I have a style and grace that are known
No one can possess since it's my very own
You too have a style that only you have the power to express
Your methods of doing things only you possess
So, the very next time someone makes an insulting remark
    to try and make you feel weak
Remember my motto, Keep right on strutting and
    turn the other cheek.....

                                   —*Anonymous*

Sisters have been guilty of whispering behind my back, "She thinks she's so much. She thinks she's white." My question is, how black is black enough? This is utter madness. All I have ever tried to do was prepare myself to succeed in life. I sacrificed and worked my butt off to climb out of the ghetto of small town Mississippi. So does that make me more "white" than black?

It's ironic. In the process, some of my own people have ostracized me for not being black enough. This is the biggest irony in the world. People "dawg" you to become a success and then ostracize you when you do. However, you are the cure to this ostracism. If no one is praising you, praise yourself. If no one wants to be with you, be by yourself. If no one has faith in you, have faith in yourself. Realize that the only opinion that matters is yours. Start blowing your own horn. Then and only then will you be content with who and where you are in life.

Dressing to impress socially is different from dressing to land a job in corporate America. The way you are dressed can make or break your career. First, you need to dress from the inside out. You have to dress and act the part. Leave the attitude at home. You don't get a second chance to make a first impression. Showcase your corporate look and let your employer know that in addition to your skills, you are a natural born leader.

*Hair

Your hair should be clean, neat and natural looking. Flashy colors and funky hairdos' are no's. Groom yourself to blend into your corporate environment. You do not want your hair to distract from your job skills.

*Make-up
  Your make-up should blend in with your complexion. It is better to have too little make-up than to have too much and look like a clown. Browns and greys generally work best on darker complexions.

*Dress
  Navy blues and greys are the traditional colors for business suits. Yours shouldn't be too tight or short. If you dress as if you are going to church, you cannot go wrong.

*Shoes
  Shoes should be clean and polished. A low to a medium heel is best. Stockings should compliment your skin tone.

*Jewelry
  Jewelry should be kept to a minimum. Invest in a nice set of pearls. Earrings and accessories should not be big and gaudy. You want to keep a nice conservative appearance.

*Perfume
  A light fragrance is the best. You don't want your co-workers to smell you from across the boardroom table.

*Nails

Nails should be clean and neat. Long nails that interfere with work should be avoided

Make an I Love Me Book

In 1996, I was promoted to captain and placed in charge of a company of 150 soldiers. About the same time, a new Colonel, big boss, came on the island. All of the company commanders were asked to come to his office so we all could chat, more like, so he could look us over. A few days after we left his office, a major pulled me aside and said, "The old man has some reservations about a female being in charge of a Military Police Company." I was in charge of the island's defense against any threat. "Oh really?" was my reply.

I called the colonel on the phone and invited him on a run. I led a brisk pace. I then began to explain that I had been a platoon leader for four years. During that time, I led soldiers into many different countries and under hostile conditions. I explained to him what my mission was, and how I would accomplish it under fire (all the time trying to run him into the ground). I then began to explain my company's shortcomings and my plans to rectify them. At the end of our run (4.5 miles), he was very tired and very impressed. He knew from my own mouth that I was extremely qualified. I had tooted the entire orchestra, and played exactly the right tune. He knew I had the Power.

I am sure if you are reading this book, you are an intelligent, lovely lady of elevated consciousness. If this is so, I am certain you have achieved and received several awards, accolades, or recommendations for the job you have now, or the jobs you have held in the past. You need to make an "I Love Me" book. In this book, you need to include a copy of your most recent resume. You need copies of your degrees or certifications. You need copies of any recommendations or glowing performance appraisals you have ever received.

This book serves two purposes. First, it will be an awesome tool to place on the table at an interview. It showcases your talents that a potential boss can physically see. Second, it will serve as a reminder. Every time you look at it, of how wonderfully talented and intelligent you are. It will be a constant reminder that. You have the Power.

SECTION THREE
ROMANCE

Chapter Seven

What Are You Looking for In a Man (where are you looking)? Be Specific, God will hear you.

I was lonely and wandering
My life had no meaning
And then came you, and a new beginning

You entered my world
And all the wrong became right
And I thank God for you each and every night

You are my heart and soul
My shelter from the cold
My darling, you complete me

So finally I feel
A true love that's real
That I used to find only in a dream

It was 1996. I sat in the theater watching Whitney Houston in "Waiting to Exhale" getting ready for a New Year's Eve Party. She was having a monologue with herself, it began "I asked God to send me a good man, and I got Robert, Kenneth and Lionel; God's got some serious explaining to do. She then says "So I got specific with God and asked can he have compassion, some sensitivity, be attractive, employed (well, you get the drift). This scene had a great impact on me. For just like Whitney's character, I kissed a long line of frogs on the way to finding my Prince Charming.

The first year after college, he had to be tall, dark, handsome, and educated. He needed to have a great job so that I could be wined and dined. The third year after college he needed to be tall, attractive and have a good job and be willing to at least go Dutch on a meal. By the fifth year after college, all he needed to be was tall (I am five/nine), employed, and have a GED. Stop the madness!

The point to this whole thing was that prior to finding my Prince Charming, I was engaged four times, but they never worked out. "Why?" you may ask. Well, now I can tell you. I was in such a rush that I was settling for less than I deserved. If the man possessed four out of nine of the characteristics I was looking for, he must be the one. Wrong!

Fiancé number one, we will designate him "The Saint," or at least he thought he was. He was attractive, gainfully employed, and wanted a family. The problem was he was also looking for a perfect woman. I was young and new, seventeen going on eighteen. He felt he could mold me into his ideal woman. He moved his sister into my dorm room, of course, to keep me company, to spy is more like it. He alienated all my friends. He gradually weaned me away from all the organizations that I was a member of. He replaced them with his band and church. On the weekends, he took me to his house so his mom could keep an eye on me.

It took me a while, but I realized that this was not love. This was an obsession. I flipped the script quickly, which you know we females can do. I said goodbye to "The Saint." Via "I DON'T NEED YOU, YOUR MONEY, YOUR CAR OR YOUR RING. ALL I NEED IS YOU OUT OF MY LIFE!" I found my power to say no.

Then came fiancé number two, we will dub him "Mr. Understanding"—which he wasn't. However, he was attractive, sensitive, and six feet tall. I was about to graduate and go into the military. He could not see himself "following me around like a puppy." It was either my dream and livelihood or him. Hmm, I thought about it for a minute and said, "SEE YA!!!!!"

We will dub fiancé number three "The Terminator." He terminated my "I love me" inoculation, at least for a little while. He was attractive, six feet tall, gainfully employed, and good in bed. But he had no sensitivity or understanding. Let's put it this way, his argument for me to take him back was, and I quote, "I have already done everything I could possibly do to you. I don't know why you won't take me back?" I replied, "You are a @#$%%! That's why." He was gone, quick, fast, and in a hurry!

Fiancé number four was crowned "The Savior." He was six feet tall, gainfully employed, had a family, and was sensitive. He was missing the other very two important characteristics. To his credit, he was a sweet man, but we differed on child rearing techniques. He felt they could do no wrong and no one should correct them but him. I felt if I was going to live in that house, the little hoodlums were going to do what I said. Soon thereafter I was out of there. He was out of my life.

Unfortunately for me, I once again met a frog. He put me through so much drama that I was forced to talk to God about all of this. I told him I was not pleased. All that I asked for in a man was that he be sensitive, attractive, a provider, understanding, at least six feet tall, gainfully employed, great in bed, and wanted a family. If he could not give me those little things, I just would not have anything else to do with men!

To show God that I meant business, I volunteered to be stationed on Johnston Island, a little island, 2 miles wide by 4 miles long. It was in the middle of the Pacific, eight hundred miles from its nearest neighbor.

I called my personnel manager to confirm. He asked me over and over again, "Are you sure that this is what you want to do." I replied, "Yes, I am sure. I am getting away from all men." I thought on an island that only had 1,200 people, 95% which are Caucasian or Polynesian, there I would be safe. Yeah, right!

You see. God was listening to my tirade. As I walked into the clinic on Johnston Island to in-process, I turned and looked at the Pharmacist and immediately fell in love. There standing before me was the finest bald head, which I find extremely sexy, chocolate brown, muscle bound, pharmacist that I had ever seen.

However, God had a sick sense of humor. I fell immediately! It took him two weeks to notice I was interested, and another six months for his feelings to catch up to mine. Was I disappointed? Oh, heck no. In that six months, I found out that he was sensitive, attractive, a provider, understanding, at least six feet tall, gainfully employed, great in bed, and wanted a family. Imagine that. A year and a half later we were married. Everyday I thank God for sending me the man that I asked for, the man that I needed. I prayed and God showed me his Awesome Power!

Chapter Eight

What Has He Done for You Lately (Today!)? What Is He Going to Be Doing Tomorrow?

When did I lose myself in you?
When will you lose yourself in me too?
When did we become one?
When did life become so much fun?
When did time begin to stand still?
When did love everlasting become real?
When did life become worth living?
When did I become so giving?
When....... will you.

Women are "Earth's" most natural born nurturer, providers, and motivators. If you are our man, the sun rises and sets on you. Once we love you, there is nothing that you could ask that we wouldn't give. Ours is a culture that has survived, because women sacrifice themselves over and over again to ensure that the ones that they love get what they need and deserve. Unconditional love is a great concept when it is a mother sacrificing over and over for her children, expecting nothing in return, but doing it because they are hers. However, when it comes to a relationship, you need to take a closer look.

If you are in a relationship with a man and you love him with all that you are, the sun rises and sets on his shoulders. You cook; you clean; you buy; you need to ask yourself, "Does he deserve it?" What did he do to deserve it in the beginning? What is he doing to deserve it now? You see adoration is a mutual agreement. If you are adoring him, he should be adoring you right back.

I am not talking about being showered with diamonds, pearls, and a Lexus. Does he come home and ask about your day? Does he call you at work or home just to tell you he loves you? Does he remember your birthday and anniversary, without your circling it on the calendar? Does he give you a massage when you are sore from the gym, or rub your feet when they are hurting from standing or walking all day, or running after his bad kids? Does he grab you for a hug, kiss you on the neck, and say, "Baby, you are my heart; I love you?"

None of the above cost a dime, but they all will show you in part or in whole if he deserves everything that you are doing for him. If your man accomplishes even half of the above, at least every now and then, if not weekly, and is contributing to your well being, he is deserving of you and your time.

However, if you are in a relationship and all of the above is only being accomplished by you, if you are the sole caretaker of your well being, it is time to reflect and ask yourself, "What has he done for me lately—today! What is he going to be doing tomorrow?" If the answer is "not a thing," then that is exactly what he should be receiving from you.

I have heard women say, "I'm looking for a man who can buy me clothes, get my nails and hair done and keep money in my pocket." Ask yourself the following; What do I bring to the table besides expectations and demands? What do I have to offer? Most men can cook and clean for themselves. It is cheaper. Why do they need a high maintenance woman to do it for them? Are you an asset or a liability for a man?

Are you sitting on a bar stool in a club waiting for a man to approach you? Chances are you'll wait all night. Men are not asking us to dance, because they know we expect a drink in return for a dance. Do you know how much he would have to spend if he bought a drink for every woman he asked to dance at a club?

Do you expect a man to foot the dinner bill every time you go out? Are you looking for a man to give you money? Hey, what's wrong with you? Why aren't you out making your own money? These days men are opting to go out with each other rather than spending a lot of money on an expensive woman.

When I dated my husband, I looked to see what he had to compliment my attributes. To my surprise, he told me, "I tallied up the pros and cons of a relationship with you." The deciding factor he said was, "You were a good girl, even though you were broke, with some potential." He saw my potential for Power.

Drama

My friends and I sit back and laugh at some of the men drama we've been through in our lives. You know, it's okay to laugh at yourself. This girl has been to the motherland and back with men. In the middle of the night in January of 1996, I scaled a nine-foot fence trying to get away from this Nigerian who was about to beat me to a pulp.

We dated for two years, but beneath the surface, I saw his potential for violence, even though he kept it under control. Like so many other women, I ignored the warning signs. In a fit of anger, he pinned me up against a wall. I could see in his eyes that he wanted to give me a good thrashing. Nonetheless, I played it cool, like I wasn't afraid. All the time I was thinking to myself, "How am I going to get out of this one?" He let me go for a moment. I ran for the door with him on my heels. I ran out of there and climbed over a nine-foot fence to safety. Believe me since that incident, I've never looked back. I finally had power over my relationships.

A friend of mine, Romesha, noticed her boyfriend was acting different. He said he had to go to work. She decided to follow him to make sure. Guess where he went? If you said over his other woman's house, you're right. She sat outside and waited until he emerged from the house. She honked her horn and told him to come over to her car. He continued to walk and told her he would see her later. She already knew about the other woman. He wasn't going to acknowledge her presence and mess up two good things.

He got in his truck and left. She chased him down the streets of Jackson, MS. He knew his way around. He made some turns and loops, until finally he lost her. She sat in the car dumbfounded over this sorry episode. A lesson learned. If you follow a man, you deserve what you get.

Another dramatic episode, Keisha heard a truck pull up outside her house. She looked to see who it was. To her surprise, it was her mother-in-law in an U-Haul with all her earthly goods in tow. She proceeded to tell her, "I'm moving in. This is my son's house." Guess what? She moved in and took over the household. A lesson learned. A house is big enough to hold only one woman. If someone has to go, it won't be me.

Tanya is flat broke. She's about to be evicted from her house, because she hasn't paid her rent. All her bills are behind. The city has turned off her water for failure to pay her twenty-dollar past due bill. She illegally turns the water on at night. In the morning, she turns it off again.

Her baby's daddy hasn't paid child support in years. He has the nerve to knock on her door in the middle of the night for a booty call. Does she let him in? You betcha. A lesson learned. If I am going to be broke, I am going to be broke by myself.

Brenda's parents were having a knock out drag down of a fight. She heard her mother tell her father, "You're sorry. You have got a little penis and can't keep it up." Later that night, she heard sounds of enjoyment coming from her parents' bedroom. Imagine that! It wasn't so small after all. A lesson learned. If you want it, just say so.

Toni lived with Leo. He hadn't given up the sex in months. All of a sudden he started laying on the charm.

Come to find out, his car had put him down. He wanted Toni to cosign for him to get another car. His credit rating was bad. She cosigned for him to get a Ford Contour. He didn't like it. Who's driving the Contour? If you guessed Toni, you're right. He's driving her Taurus. Lesson Learned. Sex can be very expensive.

Shemeeka was shocked. An acquaintance approached her and bluntly asked her, "Are you having an affair with my husband?" She told her, "I don't even know your husband." Sheemeka wanted to know what proof did the wife have to accuse her of such a thing in the first place. Sheemeka told the woman, "If you accused me of writing a bad check to go shopping, that's something I would do. Your husband is the last thing on my mind. Lesson Learned. Never ask a question you don't know the answer to. Furthermore, stop confronting other women about your husband. Heck, he lives with you. Ask him!

Chapter Nine

You Should Never Try to "Change" a Man, Compromise is the Key

Handsome and Loving
As fine as the day is long,
An extremely great provider
And a character that is strong.
You give patience and forgiveness;
You always listen to what I have to say,
You're a carpenter, electrician and a chef
And still you find time to play.
Our children will honor you in word and deed
You will be their measuring stick and gauge,
You are a confidante, a friend and teacher
And the reason we will succeed.

I learned from kissing many frogs that you cannot change a man. We go into relationships and we tell our friends "Girl, yeah, I know he smokes, but I can get him to quit." " Girl, yeah, I know he beat his last girlfriend, but I won't stand for that and I won't let him treat me that way." "Girl, yeah, I know he has a temper, but if I spend enough time with him, I can calm him down."

The sad thing is that the examples that I quoted above were statements made by my friends. One of them began to smoke, too. She ended up having a breast removed when doctors found she had breast cancer at just thirty-one years old. The other is a family member who ended up paralyzed after her husband beat her. Yes, these cases are dramatic, but they make my point. Love is not a magic wand. It will not change your partner into the perfect person after you get him to "love you enough."

Ask yourself the following questions: What do we have in common? Does this man wake-up and talk to me? Does he like to go to church? If all of the above are no, you need to say no to the relationship. Don't fool yourself into thinking you can adjust for his shortcomings. If so, you're headed for trouble. Your relationship is destined to fail. Forcing yourself to change to keep a man is not what a relationship is about. Recognize your inner power and demand nothing but the best from your man.

Keys to Successful Relationships

The first key to a healthy relationship is compromise. You have to choose your battles. If it is not important, let it slide in exchange for his giving up things you cannot live with. For example, "Yes, I can deal with the fact that you smoke, but you cannot smoke inside the house. Yes, I understand that you need to spend time with your friends, but not every Saturday night. I am going to overlook that you can't seem to get your clothes inside the hamper. But, you must learn to put the toilet seat down. Or at least leave the light on when you don't so I can tell whether it's up in the middle of the night and not end up with a butt full of "toilet water."

    I can remember slumbering to the bathroom in the middle of the night. I squatted to sit on the toilet seat. I screamed! My butt splashed into the water and hit the bottom of the bowl. I was so mad. If I told him once, I told him a thousand times to let the toilet seat down after he uses the bathroom! I had a solution to this problem. Guess what? He was going to buy me a house with two bathrooms. Today, I have my bathroom. He has his. I do not go into his bathroom for any reason, to clean or otherwise.

    However, if you met him in the club, don't be upset that he continues to go to the club. Go with him. If he was spending time with his friends when you were dating, don't expect him not to spend time with them now that you are married. Regulate the time. If he was happy with his job, goals, and status in life when you were dating him, don't expect him to suddenly adopt your dreams and goals now that you are engaged. You can encourage, but never preach and back off when asked. You have to remember that he loves you as you are. He deserves the same consideration. You have to respect his power.

    The second key to a successful relationship is the ability to communicate your wants and needs, your likes and dislikes, your hopes and dreams. We often make the mistake of putting our emotional health on the line by not communicating what we are really feeling. We hide behind safe answers. "I'm fine. Nothing's wrong. When we really want to say, I am so pissed off at you that I can't think straight. How could you be so insensitive?" Well, the answer to that question is, he can be so insensitive because you never told him how you really felt about the issue. In the interest of keeping the peace, you pasted on a smile, packed down your anger and hurt feelings.

The problem with this behavior is that after years of packing down anger and hurt feelings your bag is going to get full. You will explode. Your unsuspecting mate will have forgotten to take out the trash that you asked him to take out the night before. You come home and see it, still sitting there in the kitchen. Years of pressed down feelings begin to pour out on his head. Trash that could have been ignored is now grounds for divorce. You are going off on him, the kids, and even the dog. They are all standing still, afraid to move. They are praying they will live to see tomorrow.

All this? Just because the trash was not taken out? No, what this is really about is your not communicating your true feelings when you felt them. If there is something you simply cannot tolerate (for me, it's that old left-up toilet seat), let him know up front. If he does or says something to hurt your feelings, take a couple of minutes to calm down (so you don't cuss him out). Then, let him know calmly that what he said hurt you and would he please not say or do it again.

If your mate knows your wishes, wants and desires and still does not fulfill them, shame on him. However, if you are hoping that your wishes, wants and desires will reach him through osmosis, and you haven't told him, shame on you. Telling (communication) is the key.

Chapter Ten

How Will a Man Help You Attain Your Goals?

Early in life, so much importance is placed on having a man. The moment a girl reaches dating age, everyone wants to know who's her boyfriend? Quality is not the measuring instrument. Having one is enough. No matter how he treats you, family members look down on you if you do not have that male appendage attached to your side.

When I was in college, no one asked, "How are your grades?" It was always, "Who is your boyfriend?" I was a serious student. I did not need the added distraction of a man. The thought of getting saddled with a baby was an instant turn off. Most women don't rebound mentally after having an unexpected baby. Your goals are put on the back burner for the benefit of your child. I watched my sister get pregnant at fifteen and eighteen. She graduated from college, but life was not easy. I made up my mind that I would educate myself and stop the cycle of teen pregnancy in my immediate family. You have to set priorities if you want to acquire the power.

Women are looking for that big pie in the sky. We all say we want a man who's educated, has a good job, who's nice, religious and understanding. But are we being honest with ourselves? The truth is, if he looks okay and the sex is slamming, we fall hook, line and sinker. Business is ruled by money. Relationships are driven by sex and sexuality.

You Have the Power

At the beginning of a relationship, all a man is looking for is sex. Don't lay your body on the table. Unfortunately, most women are so insecure and feel they have to give up the sex to keep a man's attention. But stall the sex for as long as you can. If sex is all that he wants, it won't take long for his true colors to show. Getting a man is not hard. Keeping a man is.

It's amazing how easy women fall prey to a smooth man. All he has to do is tell us a joke and make us smile, take us to see a love movie and sex us good. We are happy as a lark. The moment something goes wrong, we start complaining that he's a "scrub", a.k.a. a man living at home with his parents without a job. We're disappointed that he didn't change overnight. Hey, you can't take a person with an up and down ragged life and instantly make him perfect. Wasn't he living at home with his parents when you met him? Wasn't he self-employed, a.k.a. in-between jobs, when you met him? You chose to ignore those warning signals, so why are you complaining now?

When I worked as a child support attorney, I remembered women coming to see me in a fit of anger. They wanted to know why their child support check was late. My question was, "Did he have a job when you met him?" If the answer was no, why on earth did you have a baby for him? Was he in-between jobs when you met him? If he was, how are we supposed to make him get a job? It's a little too late to start complaining after you've had a child.

Ladies, we are placing too much importance on sex in choosing a mate. Don't trade the vital characteristics that a relationship needs to thrive for sex. Communicate with your mate. Tell him what makes you feel good in bed. You can teach each other to be great lovers. You can tell your mate how to touch your body. You cannot tell him to get a job. You can tell your mate how to kiss your breast. You cannot tell him to be a responsible man. You can tell your mate how hard or how fast. You cannot tell him how to love you. Work together. Both of you can have a fulfilling sex life. Your relationship will have power.

I noticed Sandra, a friend of mine was not her usual happy go lucky self. Nothing unusual was going on. Sure, we had our usual complaints about being over worked and under paid. That wasn't anything new. I figured it must be serious. If she wanted me to know, eventually, she would tell me. I was walking by her office one day. Sandra called me in and said she needed to talk. She confided she was in a love triangle. She was living with her boyfriend of two years. The problem was he had no vision or goals for the future. Anything they did or acquired was at her insistence. He was divorced with three children. He lived in her trailer. He drove her car. They used her credit to buy things. He brought nothing to the table besides being a nice guy.

Now an ex-boyfriend had called and asked her to marry him. She said, "I shouldn't even be thinking about it, but I am." This guy had his stuff together, and had plans for the future. She wanted my advice on what she should do. I told her she had to look at the inside and outside of both men and visualize what path she wanted her life to take. Look at where each man was in his life. What was his goals in life? How did her goals compare to his? If you are the only one with goals, you may need to move on. Life's too short to waste on a train going no where. Use your power, shed the excess baggage, and move on!

Sharonda recently divorced her husband of three years. We had lunch at a local restaurant in Hattiesburg. She talked about the divorce and how she met him. I asked her, "What did you know about him before you married him?" She replied, "We talked on the phone. He was a nice guy. I got lost in the moment."

Check your mate out. If you want to get a job, don't you check out the company you're interested in? You study its assets and liabilities. Financial stability is important. The past ten years of performance are vital to projected future performance. Why are we not doing this when we choose a life time mate? You need to ask about his past sexual history. To verify, ask to see his HIV card. If he doesn't have one, both of you go get one. You need to ask to see his credit report. You don't want to marry someone and then find out his credit is so bad a store won't lend him money to buy a pair of shoes. Ask to see his tax returns. These are basic things you need to know before you say "I do." If they are negative, you need the information so you can be equipped with the power to say, "I don't." Now you are exercising power over your future.

Chapter Eleven

Love Builds Relationships, Respect Sustains Marriages

My husband and I grew up in the same neighborhood in Grenada. He lived on one side of the track. I lived on the other side. He was my older brother's friend. He left Grenada in 1983 to become a big, bad marine.

In 1995, I saw him at a local club. Our eyes met across the room. He was six-three, fine, tall, dark, and so sexy. He came over and said, "Hello, the last time I saw you, you were running around with a snotty nose." I thought to myself, "Well, buddy, when I get finished with you, my nose will be the last thing you will be thinking about."

We danced the night away. When the club closed, he asked me, "Do you want to go to breakfast at Shoney's." I said, "Sure." He left for a moment to tell his brother where he was going. As soon as he got out of sight, I took that moment to high tail it out of there. Breakfast at three a.m., in plain English, is a booty call. Thanks, but, no thanks.

The next day, I was talking to a friend and asked her, "Do you know who is going to be my husband?" She looked at me and said, "Who?" When I told her, she just laughed. I told her, "You just wait and see." It was an odd thing to say. He was stationed in North Carolina. I lived in Houston, Texas. I headed back later in the afternoon. I thought nothing more of it. Over the next couple of months, every time I went to Grenada, I would ask his brother about him.

In January of 1996, I moved to Jackson, Mississippi. Where one day out of the blue, he called me on the phone. It thought to myself, what does he want (as if I didn't know).

He called to tell me that he was going to be stationed in Hattiesburg, Mississippi, a small city just ninety miles south of Jackson. He wanted to stop by on his way from Hattiesburg to Grenada (Jackson sits midway between Grenada and Hattiesburg. I told him, "Sure, why not."

The moment I saw him again, I knew he was the man for me. I quickly assessed his portfolio. He had a secure job, thirteen years in the military. He came from a good family. He was single with good credit. I thought to myself, "This dude looks very promising. I think I'll keep him."

December of 1996, I was in the clouds. The wedding I fantasized about since childhood was about to happen. I was about to live happily ever after. I was so caught up in having the perfect wedding I was making everyone around me sick. I stressed myself out and came down with a bad case of laryngitis. My mother pulled me aside and said, "Girl, you're getting on my last nerve." But even after all of that stressing, the wedding went without a hitch.

Now the reception, that was another matter all together. It was supposed to be booze free, but as the night wore on, beer and whiskey started coming out of the wood work. In the back of my mind I thought, "These river rats are going to get drunk and tear this place up and I'm going to have to pay for it." I went to talk to my new husband about the situation. To my amazement, he was drinking too. I proceeded to tell him,

"You know there is no drinking. You need to tell everyone to put their bottles away." He looked at me as if I were crazy. I'm sure he was thinking, "This girl is tripping."

His sister overhearing our conversation piped in, "You see, she's bossing you already. Look what you've gotten yourself into. You should have waited!" At the same time, I was thinking to myself, "What have I gotten myself into!"

Our wedding night was not spent making wild passionate love. My new husband left as soon as the reception was over to confront his sister. She was not home so he talked to his mother instead. He told her what his sister said and his mother took his sister's side, telling him, "Well, you should have waited." He in turn told his mother, "If you had doubts, you should have mentioned them before I got married. I would have waited but it's my wedding night and you can keep it to yourself now." His father, who was silent up to this point, finally said, "That's right."

From that night on, I never had any problems with my mother-in-law. I am by no means saying that we instantly became like mother and daughter but we respected each other. If we didn't have anything positive to say to each other, we kept it to ourselves or whispered behind the other's back.

Marriage is like a double edged sword. In the beginning, everything you do seems to be wrong. You're trying to deal with a new marriage. At the same time, you have to include your families so they don't feel left out. Women generally call their mothers every day. Most men don't believe in making phone calls. You have to make that extra effort and call your husband's family. You have to make that extra effort to remember your mother-in-law's birthday. Your husband has a hard enough time remembering yours. When you send your mother a mother's day card, remember to send his mother one, too.

I know you're saying, "This woman has lost it." Why should I continue to respect his family when they don't respect me? No, it's not easy. It's called keeping the peace for the sake of your marriage and it's worth the extra effort. It took me a year into my marriage to realize this. My mother-in-law died two years into our marriage. I miss her and wish I had tried harder to establish a mother-daughter relationship with her.

I have several friends whose mothers-in-law have made their lives a living hell. Nobody is good enough for a mother's son. Your husband cannot sit back and watch you two duke it out. To cut out the confusion, a son has to step in and say, "Hey Mom, this is my wife. It is important to me that the two women I love get along. I am committed to making my marriage work. I need you to work with us." You both have the power, you need to cooperate and graduate.

Respect Each Other

I've had several friends say, "You're so submissive to your husband." I had one go so far as to say she was going to school me on how to handle him. Little do they know that my husband submits to me too. You have to pick and choose your battles. You can't blow up over everything.

Most divorces don't occur because partners do not love each other. They occur because couples stop respecting each other. Couples start to argue about money and children. One blames the other for not handling his share of the load. When you start to say something ugly and hurtful, stop right there. Tell your mate, "We need a cooling off period."

I have seen women blatantly disrespect a man in public. That's a no, no and disrespectful. You have to learn to watch your mouth, because once you say something, you can't take it back. It's like a round down range. (That's military lingo) Once you fire it, you can't take it back. A man has to feel like a man. I try not to belittle or embarrass my husband in front of others.

As a man, he has enough to contend with. I once heard someone say, "Couples shouldn't go to bed upset." I say if you're going to say something spiteful, you need to go to bed and cool off. Sleep on it. Things will be clearer in the morning. Exercise power over your mouth. You will learn when to shut up.

Keep Your Family Out of Your Business

I have a girlfriend who has been married for five years. She is black, her husband is white. Whenever she goes home to visit her family, he never travels with her. I found this strange so I asked her, "Does your family have a problem with your being married to a white man?" "No, she replied. My sister is dating a white man. My brother is living with a white woman."

I then asked, "Well, why doesn't your husband ever go home with you?' She said, "My family doesn't like him, but I don't know why." As we talked, I asked her if she ever put him on the phone to talk to her mother or siblings? She said, "No." I learned the only time her siblings or mother heard any information about her husband was when she called home to complain about how mad he made her or about what he was not doing in the house. I asked her how did she expect them to like him? They only hear negative things about him. That is the only impression they have of him. She sat looking at me with her mouth open. It dawned on her that what I was saying was true.

It's okay to tell family members things, but some things you need to keep inside your house. They can offer you advice but they should never confront your spouse or tell him what he needs to be doing. Remember. Couples have short memories when it comes to their arguments. Family members have a hard time forgetting.

While I was in ROTC, a new professor of military science was hired. He was a Lieutenant Colonel. This man knew he had it going on! When he drove on campus in his coal black beamer, our mouths would be hanging open; every girl started plotting in her mind how to get his attention. He was quick to tell us that he was happily married. Soon thereafter, I found out, he meant every word.

During the first two weeks at his new job, he found his wife, who was a teacher, a job. Then he bought her a house in the town where she would be working. He took the thirty-mile commute to his job. He proceeded to furnish the home to her specifications. All she had to do was fly in and unpack her suitcase. He brought her to every function. He introduced her as the love of his life. She was cool, but polite. As the year progressed, he started coming to work depressed. One day I inquired, "What is the problem?" He told us, "I am getting separated." Soon, thereafter, he got divorced. What you ask was the problem? Well, it seems her single girlfriends convinced her there was no way he was working on a campus with all those "pretty young girls" and not cheating on her. She then took this conversation to her bitter, divorced sister. Her sister said, "You need to divorce him." She let her single friends and her single sister talk her out of her marriage. Because of their accusations, she became suspicious and uncertain. This man was crazy about his wife. He continued to pay the note on the house and car for the next four years. Instead of checking out the facts, she accepted the fiction. She ended up losing her self-confidence and her husband.

A friend of mine found out that her husband was cheating. He was in the military and went ahead of the family to get their household set up, but she found out that he not only set up their household, but was playing house with a twenty-year-old and squandered all of their money on her. Every time I saw my friend, she was crying. I wanted to scream and tell her to pull her self together. She vowed to make her marriage work and stayed with him. They had two children and she did not want her children to be without their father. So, "for better or worse" kicked in. No matter what she did, like a magnet, he gravitated toward the younger woman. Whenever, the girl would call their home, he would go running. It took him a year to finally realize that this girl only wanted his money. Two years later and after much counseling, my friend and her husband found their way back to each other.

To stay or not to stay, it's a question that only you can answer. If you decide to stay, you need counseling to deal with the feelings of betrayal and help you regain trust in your mate. There are things that both of you probably can improve on so you can gain power over your marriage.

Don't be dismayed if you find yourself arguing with your spouse. Disagreements between husband and wife are inevitable. If you're together, you are going to disagree about how something should be done, or what each of you should be doing or how I perceive you are treating me; this is normal. If you never have disagreements, you probably do have a problem. It may mean that one partner is internalizing and sacrificing his or her happiness, all in the name of getting along. Arguments usually occur when changes are needed and when behaviors, thoughts, and feelings need to be reexamined. Don't be afraid to confront your mate about what is bothering you. If you deal with conflict positively, your marriage can benefit after the argument is over. Making up can stimulate your marriage.

Ground Rules for Marital Disputes

1. Start right. Set a time to discuss the problem, a convenient time for you and your mate. Avoid bringing up the problem, when your mate is in the middle of watching football. He will tune you out.

2. Set aside your desire to "Win." Winning an argument is just like winning a battle. It does not mean you are going to win the war. Saving your marriage should be your first priority. It takes two to make a marriage and likewise, it takes two to destroy a marriage.

3. Avoid blaming each other. Assessing blame only makes the other party defensive and breaks down communication.

4. Ask your mate to role play. Stand in the other person's shoes and try to see how he feels.

5. Don't make personal attacks. For example, if you say, "You need to pick up behind yourself. You are such a lazy slob." It will only lead to defensiveness. You will get nothing resolved. Instead say, "I wish you wouldn't leave your clothes in the middle of the floor." You will get a more positive response.

6. Don't psychoanalyze your mate. No one wants to feel like he's being examined by a shade tree shrink.

7. If your mate starts to fight unfairly, you need to stop the discussion immediately. Tell him we will talk about this later.

8. Don't put your mate on the spot by insisting on an answer then and now. Give him time to absorb what you said. Schedule a time when you all can revisit the subject.

"When Mother Theresa received her Nobel Prize, she was asked, "What can we do to promote world peace?" She replied, "Go home and love your family."

Have you ever felt like taking an escape from the everyday grind of life? Have you ever wanted to run away and forget all of your problems. It sounds tempting at a glance, but then you start to think, "What about the children? Who will take care of them?" Who will take care of the house? If you let them, the responsibilities of life will suck you up. They can make you a very bitter person.

I remember when I was four months pregnant with my second child. I was feeling burnt out. I couldn't rest, because I had a six-month-old child at home to take care of. The daycare called one day to tell me Trey was running a fever. I took off work to take him to the doctor. The doctor examined him and said, "Trey's fine. You're the one that looks terrible." He proceeded to prescribe medicine for me. My husband, bear in mind, who is in the military stationed in another state told me, "I don't know why you're stressed out. What's so hard about getting our son up and taking him to daycare? Keep in mind this was something he had never done? I wanted to scream but instead, I packed up my anger for another day.

To make life easier on me, I hired an in-home sitter so I wouldn't have to take off work when the children were sick or spend extra time shuttling them off to the daycare in the mornings. My husband had the nerve to ask, "Why do you need an in-home sitter?" I'm saying to myself, "Listen block head, we have no family in town. What happens if the children are sick? Who has to stay home with them? I refuse to be stressed out by you or anyone else."

You have to make life as easy as possible for yourself. When you have children, make sure you are prepared to be their primary caretaker. Don't disillusion yourself. The chores of parenting will never be fifty/fifty. One will give more for the financial well-being of the child, while the other, gives more intangible things. Both are very important. Know what your role is in your family so you can have the power to make your marriage work.

A successful marriage, just like beauty, is in the eye of

the beholder. One person's idea of what marriage is and should be, may be different from someone else's views. Marriage is an institution in and of itself. Two people have to be committed to making their marriage work. Growth and mutual respect are needed for the relationship to flourish. If the grass looks greener on the other side of the fence, perhaps you should water your own yard more frequently.

You have to realize love is a decision, not a feeling. You have to "decide" in your heart and head, this person is the only person you want to be with for the rest of your life. It is the decision to love each other that helps you clean up after your spouse when he has a nasty flu. It is the decision to love that will allow you to forgive each other when you have crossed the line. It is the decision to love that will keep your spouse there, even if you are incapacitated.

When you are unhappy in your marriage, don't look for other people to make you feel complete. You need to nurture, support and cherish the person you made vows to. Marriage is a tough road. However, the rewards are far more gratifying than anyone can imagine if the couple is united in love, faith and commitment.

Chapter Twelve

Stroke Your Man's Ego

Once you get married, don't forget the things you did to get that man. You need to continue to make him feel special. If you sexed him five times a week before marriage, he will expect it at least three times a week after you get married. If you greeted him at the door with a kiss, you need to keep it up. If you romanced him with candlelight dinners, you need to cook him one every now and then.

We get relaxed after we get married. We stop doing the things we did to attract our mate in the first place. It gets worse after the children come. You've worked all day, picked the children up from daycare, and cooked dinner. You barely have time to think about your own happiness and well-being let alone your spouse's. Your children need both parents to be happy. Therefore, you have to do things to keep that man and make him feel special. When you see the sparks start to dim, you need to jumpstart the engine before it's too late. Ignite the power in your relationship.

When I was a little girl, one day I was eavesdropping on grown folks conversations. I overheard my aunt talking to one of my older cousins who was about to get married. She took her aside and said, "I am going to give you some advice that has sustained my marriage. Never tell a man no. When Ed says screw, I screw." That was all I heard before someone came along and asked me what was I doing listening to grown folks conversations. However, that stuck with me for years before I even knew what she meant.

Ladies, I know sometimes the days are long and hard. You work ten hours. You come home and have to work for at least another three. Finally, you go to bed and feel something poking you in your back. Your first inclination is to play sleep. But, the thing is persistent. It just will not stop poking you. You then decide you will just turn over and say, "Not tonight, I have a headache. Don't do it. Here's why.

Sex does not always mean I am horny. Sometimes sex means, I have had a hard day. I need to unwind. Sometimes sex means, the whole world was against me today. I need to feel that you are with me. Sometimes sex means, I love you so much. I can't take it. I need to express it physically. Sometimes sex is I just want to be close to you. And yes, sometimes sex means, you are so fine and sexy I just need to take you right here and now!

The issue is you never know which of the above your man is feeling. If you tell him no, you may be contributing to the stressors, the negativity or the "you ain't nothing," that the world has told him all day. I know this will not be easy, especially when all you want to do is fall asleep. However, the rewards you reap will be well worth it. Try it for a week. You just might like it!

Love Savers

Each day say, "I love you to you and then to your partner."

Be grateful for your mate (remember when you didn't have one).

Write down your greatest hopes for your love relationship and place the slip of paper inside a book of spiritual inspiration.

Make a fearless and searching moral inventory of yourself. Ask yourself, What more can I do to make my mate happy? Then, do it.

When your mate gets out of the shower, tell him how sexy he is, i.e., "Dag baby, when I see you naked, I can't stay mad at you."

Write love notes and slip them in your mate's pocket, briefcase, etc. When he is having a hard day and opens his briefcase, he will be pleasantly surprised and grateful that you love him so much.

Everyone loves to be surprised. Light candles; Get a sitter; and seduce your mate.

Make love coupons. That say, "This one entitles you to a kiss. This one entitles you to one fantasy, etc.

Be creative in bed. Take the initiative when it comes to sex. When you initiate sex, he feels irresistible. The feeling is stronger than when he initiates it. You must nourish His Power!

SECTION FOUR
THE FINANCIAL

Chapter Thirteen

Girl, You Need to Handle Your Business

A comedian once said, "The difference between being broke and poor is when you're poor you don't have anything. When you're broke, you have a lot of stuff you cannot afford." We waste our hard earned dollars on expensive cars, clothes, and Air Jordans. So much importance is being placed on acquiring these material things that children are robbing and killing each other to get them. Our philosophy is buy what you want and beg for what you need. People generally have more month left at the end of the money.

You can be assured of two things in life: death and taxes. Before you get your paycheck, Uncle Sam gets his money up front. Most people are not preparing themselves financially for the future. Our minds are on the here and now. We're leaving the future to take care of itself. You have a better chance of starving to death at 65 than of dying before retirement. If you are not preparing for the future, you will probably live long enough to become a burden on your children.

Vanessa and I are not accountants or investment brokers. We are two women who lived off credit cards, spent money on three hundred dollar phone bills (chatting with each other), and never owned a thing. Thank God for my Officer Basic Course instructor who took me to an investment seminar. I must admit I only went initially for the free steak and Mississippi Mud Pie dinner. However, as the evening went on, I listened to other former military personnel, who now helped people invest for a living. The concept that they quoted was not difficult. "Pay yourself first." An IRA (individual retirement account) tops out at $166.66 a month. That is the maximum you can invest every month.

How many of us blow that much eating out and going to the movies in a month's time (I know I did easily, on two hour conversations to Vanessa in Houston). So how difficult is it to start an allotment and have that same amount automatically deducted each pay period between now and 65. Yes, you may have to sacrifice going out and buying that wicked outfit. However, when you are 65 and don't have to depend on your children for your well-being and livelihood, it will be well worth the sacrifice. In this day and age, let's face it, money is Power.

Common Money Mistakes

If you have an automobile that costs more than your house, you're wrong.

If you have an expensive car and live with your parents, and you are not saving your money, you're trifling.

If you live in a mobile home and have a satellite dish in the back yard and a Cadillac sitting in your front yard, you're trifling.

If you're getting your hair and nails done on a weekly basis and are not paying your bills, you're wrong.

If you're getting your hair and nails done on a weekly basis and are wearing designer clothes, and your kids are dressed in rags (or even bargain brands), you're trifling.

If your FUBU and Tommy Gear are your top investments, you're wrong.

If you have gold teeth, a gold chain, a gold bracelet and don't have money saved in the bank, you're wrong.

Regina's parents are in their late seventies and are both in poor health. Her father is bedridden from multiple strokes and her mother is battling advanced Alzheimer's. Her family has hired around the clock sitters to care for them. Regina has problems finding reliable sitters, so she often has to take off work to take care of them. She tightly budgets the money for her parents' sitters and living expenses. Her family can't afford to pay money for her parents' health care expenses. Both of her parents retired from good-paying jobs. She was amazed that their life savings amounted to only $20,000 dollars. It was not nearly enough to supplement their retirement and social security for a year. Regina commented one day, "Even that wash woman managed to save more money than that."

The woman Regina was referring to was the late Miss Oseola McCarthy. Miss McCarthy was a wash woman who, from her life's savings donated $150,000 dollars to the University of Southern Mississippi. How did a woman who made so little save so much money? As you might imagine, she did not make much money from each load of those clothes she did but by doing so many loads of clothes, the money added up over time. I heard a tale around Hattiesburg that she saved money religiously all of her life. She did not know that she could withdraw money from her savings account. Many of us should borrow that philosophy. We should think of our own savings as untouchable.

Ms. McCarthy is a good example of compound interest working at its best. She knew how to make her money work for her. She lived below her means in a very modest home. She saved and tucked her money away in the bank. Your money cannot work for you if you let a car salesman talk you into spending it on a shiny new car. The insurance alone is going to put a huge dent in your pocket book. Cars do not appreciate in value, they began depreciating from the moment you drive them off the lot. Your money cannot work for you if you let Foot Locker talk you into paying outrageous prices for shoes. Your money cannot work for you if you spend it all on acquiring the latest in Tommy Gear. You have to keep as much of your money as possible. Invest it! Make it work for your future and your family's.

I know you're thinking again, "These women are tripping." That's a fair question. But consider this, a lot of people are practicing this theory and leaving wealth for their children. They are getting richer while most people are getting poorer. Take notes and stop wasting your money on a lot of stuff you can't afford, or don't really need.

Just about any one can invest twenty dollars a month. A lot of companies have plans where the money can be deducted from your checking account. Each dollar is a commitment to your children's future. Do not touch it for any reason. It's not easy, but you can do it if you discipline yourself. Then you can sit back and watch your money grow.

Money Saving Tips

Move in with your parents, but you need to save your money to pay off your bills.

If you are getting your hair done once a week, you may need to get it done once a month. To save even more money, do home relaxers (Oh, but no, we wouldn't dream of doing that). Go to the beauty shop every three months for a cut and trim.

If you are getting your nails done once a month, do them your self. You can purchase all the equipment at a beauty supply store.

Cut down on your shopping trips. Go to the store only when it is absolutely necessary.

Bad Credit

In college, my finances got really bad. I did the credit card juggle. I would alternate monthly payments between the companies, just trying to hold my ground. But, you know it's really bad when you stop answering the telephone. One Saturday morning as I was lying in bed, the phone rang. I thought to myself, "It could only be a friend or a family member at seven a.m. so I answered the phone. The caller said in a friendly voice, "Hey, how are you doing." I was half asleep so I couldn't quite catch the voice. and replied, "Fine." Then, the kind lady proceeded to tell me who she was and why she was calling. I knew I was caught! The dreaded Visa company had finally caught me at home. This was prior to caller I.D. But these days, we're one up on those creditors!

You hear people talk all the time about not being able to purchase a home because of bad credit. We all have periods in our life where we have fallen on hard times, but having bad credit is not the end of the world. You need to deal with the delinquent accounts. Remember, a slow pay is better than not paying at all. Slowly start to pay those old bills off and do not incur any additional bills. Once those old bills are paid off, slowly start getting small accounts with stores that you can pay off within a month. Pay consistently. You are on your way to starting a new credit history. Over time, the new history will offset the negative impact of your past history. Restart your Power.

A person's biggest investment is their home. It takes years of establishing good credit to qualify for a home. You enter into a loan for twenty or thirty years. By the time you finish paying for the house, you pay three times the amount you borrow. Why is it that people neglect their biggest investment?

Most times, you can pass by a house and know a trifling person lives there. The house is in utter despair. Three beat up cars are parked on an overgrown lawn in the front of the house. Two are somehow working and one is on bricks. A couch and old stove are on the front porch. Clothes are hung out to dry on the front porch, and you wonder why your neighbors are complaining and don't want you living in the same neighborhood with them?

My husband and I were full of excitement with the purchase of our first home. I immediately bought a lawn mower, hedge trimmer and an edger so he could keep the yard up. He would go out and cut the grass and return in twenty minutes and the yard looked like a twenty minute job, too. The lawn wouldn't be edged nor the hedges trimmed. You could tell the person who had done that yard took no pride in the job. On the other hand, he would go out and spend two hours washing his car until it glistened like new. I'll admit our yard was the worst kept on the block. I knew my neighbors were probably saying, "There goes the neighborhood!" I got tired of constantly nagging my husband to do the lawn after the grass got two feet tall. Eventually, I gave up and just hired someone to do the yard. As we arrived home one day, my husband commented, "Our yard looks good!" I thought to myself, "No thanks to you!" I finally had to admit that yard work was not one of his many attributes.

I had a friend who lived in a pristine neighborhood where all the houses were immaculate with perfectly kept lawns. Like me, she had to constantly nag her husband to do their yard. He let their yard get so over grown that their neighbor even came over on several occasions to cut their grass. I know he was cursing as he mowed it. Oh, he didn't do it to be neighborly. It was his way of telling them, "You need to get off your butt and cut your grass." She and her husband got upset. How would you feel if a snide neighbor came over and mowed your lawn? My friend and her husband got very upset and wanted to go and confront their neighbor, but what could they say, "I'm so upset, because you came over and cut my over grown lawn?" This guy was protecting his investment and had they kept their yard cut, he wouldn't have had to come over and do it for them in the first place.

Invest in the upkeep of your neighborhood. A neighborhood is appraised by the outside conditions of houses. The inside is your own personal business. Use your power to protect your investment.

Home Faux Pas

Don't park cars in your front yard.

Don't do your mechanic work in your front yard.

Don't use your front porch for storage of old refrigerators and stoves.

Don't move your old sofa from your den to your front porch.

Paint your house at least every fifteen years.

Don't let your grass grow taller than your children before you cut it.

Don't hang your laundry to dry on your front porch

Friends and Money Don't Mix

I had a friend from college. She was my ace. We were inseparable. We were joined at the hip. It was like if you pinched her, I yelled, "Ouch!" The year was 1996, she called me all distraught. Her car was in need of repairs and she had no funds. She wanted to borrow $250.00 dollars. And oh, by the way, she asked, "Can you send it by Western Union?" This being my ace and all, I said, It'll be there in an hour." She replied, "I'll pay you back in thirty days."

After I'd sent the money, she did not call to say she'd received it. So, I called her house to make sure. Her husband answered the phone and told me, "Yes, she received the money. She's gone to the auto mechanic already." After that, he hung up. That was it. No thank you, no nothing. I waited around thinking that she might call me later, but she never did.

Fast forward to the present, five years later in 2001. I still have not heard from her. I called on the birth of her second child, when she suffered a miscarriage, and on holidays. I got her answering machine. My calls were never returned. Now, I am pissed but not about the money. I mean, this was my ace, but for almost five years, she has not called. Why? Because, she fears that I will ask her for the money. Now really, how tired is that?

I loaned another friend $250.00 when she said she would return it the next week when she received her pay check. I did not hear from her the next week so I tried calling her. Her number had been changed to an unlisted one. In fact, it took two years before I heard from her again. She got my number from directory assistance in Houston, TX. Several people had the same name. She was persistent in trying to find me. When I talked to her, I asked her if she remembered she owed me money. She replied, "I thought I paid you back." She sent me my money. I lost a good friend for two years over money. I don't ever want this to happen again.

As a result of these incidents I don't lend what I cannot comfortably afford to give away. You can call this advice, or a warning: If you lend money to friends, don't expect to get it back . Don't sit and count the days until they said they were going to return it. I have been burned too many times lending money and expecting to receive it back. If they return it, just let it be a pleasant surprise.

I have a girlfriend who will tell you outright, "I am a shopaholic. I can't help myself." She lives to go to the mall. Recently, she started working on her masters degree which she said was going to help cut out her shopping. She figured that she'd be too busy studying. She also needed money for her tuition. I was right on the verge of offering to lend her the money, but I decided to stand back and think about it for a couple of days. Later, she and I were on the phone when she told me that she had been to the mall and bought something. "Hmmm," I thought to myself, "If she could go to the mall and waste her money, she could also pay her tuition. She would have to learn to prioritize. Mean while, my money was staying in my pocket while she would have to gain power over her own finances.

Chapter Fourteen

Insure Your Family's Future

I heard about a model insuring her body for a billion dollars. Some people said, "She must be crazy." I thought, "You go girl!" To me, it was a great investment, because she was protecting her future, which for her, was her body. I mean, what if she fell and broke a hip on a photo shoot? How would she live? Rarely will you hear an agent try to sell you disability insurance. Still there is a significant likelihood that you will be out of work for a prolonged period due to an illness or accident. Therefore, thre's a great likelihood that you'll need such insurance. Sure it's expensive. But if you can afford disability insurance on your job, get it. You'll want to have power over your financial future should you become disabled and are unable to work.

I remember an insurance agent coming to our house collecting money for insurance. He ingratiated himself into our family. He wanted us to think he was looking out for our best interest. But look, insurance agents are in the business of making money. Don't be fooled into thinking that your agent is your "friend". He is not looking out for your family as much as he is trying to sell you whatever is going to make him the most profit. He wants to convince you to purchase whole life insurance. You get the gimmick, "Well you can collect money from your policy. You can't collect money under a term life policy." Bear in mind, that is not the purpose of insurance. If you want to save money, invest it or put it in the bank. If an agent only sold term life insurance, he would starve to death. He gets more profits in selling you whole life insurance at an outrageous price.

Are you properly insuring your family? If you died tomorrow, how would your family be impacted. Would your spouse be able to meet the family's needs on his/her salary? Your family needs to be adequately insured so that if anything happens to you or your spouse, there is money to meet funeral expenses and take care of your children. You don't want to put your family in a financial crisis.

How much death insurance do you need? How much can you afford? Can you imagine a young family with three kids? They have $50,000 worth of life insurance. What would happen if the breadwinner died? His income is vital to support the family. Is this enough money to take care of this family? No, the family would be flat broke within two years.

If you have children, you need enough insurance to support them until they are eighteen. To keep a young family going, you need between $200,000—$500,000 worth of insurance. Whether you get whole life or term insurance is up to you. Just be sure you have adequate insurance to protect your family.

What happens if you and your family are involved in a serious accident. The other driver has minimal insurance. Your injuries exceed his policy limits. If the person is underinsured, chances are he probably does not have money to compensate you out of his pocket. You can sue, but the old adage, "You can't get blood from a turnip" kicks in. If he doesn't have anything, you can't get anything. How is your family compensated? What do you do? You have to protect your family from uninsured drivers. Dollar for dollar, the minimal amount of insurance costs more than a larger policy. Did you know that you pay more for auto insurance if you get the minimal deductible. What you need to do is up your deductible. Put the money aside that you save for an emergency. If your automobile is paid for, change from full coverage to liability. You need uninsured motorist protection. It protects you and your family if you are in an accident with an uninsured motorist. Your insurance premium will be cut in half. If your college student is in a car accident while riding with a friend who does not have insurance, your uninsured motorist coverage will kick in and pay for his injuries. I represented a four year old who was riding in a car with his step-mother. She ran a stop sign and ran into another driver. The child suffered a broken arm. She did not have insurance. The child's mother had uninsured motorist protection. We were able to collect for his injuries under his mother's policy.

I represented a family whose mother was killed in a bus accident. One night a drunk driver ran a stop sign and hit the bus. The bus flipped over. My clients' mother was thrown out of the bus. It landed on top of her. She was killed instantly. The drunk driver did not have insurance. We collected under the bus owner's uninsured motorist policy. Her family gained financial power.

I also represented a young, black college girl. She was dating a white guy who took out some life insurance over the phone. He told the insurance representative he wanted to leave the proceeds to his wife, Tameeka. He later told Tameeka that if anything happened to him, he wanted her taken care of. He died several months later in a car accident.

His parents tried to get the insurance proceeds from the insurance company, but the insurance company would not release the funds siting that he mentioned a wife. His parents told them that he was never married. They came to Tameeka asking her to sign papers that stated she was not married to John. She refused to do it. We offered to split the proceeds with the parents, but they said flatly "no". They said in turn, that they would give us one thousand dollars. We told them, "We'll see you in court."

The insurance company then deposited the one hundred thousand dollars of insurance proceeds into the court. Who do you think John wanted to receive the proceeds? Who do you think the court granted the proceeds to? If you guessed Tameeka, you're wrong. The court ruled that John's intent was to leave the proceeds to Tameeka only if they were married. The parents walked away with a fat one hundred grand. Tameeka, as before, was left a broke college student. This all could have been prevented if John would have made his intentions clear and exercised power over the distribution of his insurance proceeds.

Chapter Fifteen

My Will Be Done

If you ask the average woman why she does not have a will, she will probably tell you, "I don't have anything worth putting in one." My response to that is you can't afford to not have a will. If you have a husband and children, you want to spell out how you want your property distributed. You would be amazed at the things people find to fight over when a family member dies.

Reasons You Need a Will

1. You will eventually die.

2. You are married/divorced/widowed.

3. You have children.

4. You own cars, home, or personal property.

5. You own bank accounts.

6. You have stocks and bonds.

7. You have a company pension plan.

8. Your financial circumstances have changed.

9. Your health has changed.

10. You intend to disinherit a family member.

I have prepared wills for several clients. I show them the "boiler plate" will. I advise them to list all of their assets down to the kitchen sink and how they want them distributed. Oftentimes, they do not want to be bothered with this. They say, "My children can divide the property in equal shares." What they are doing is giving their children something to argue about when they die. You need to exercise power over the distribution of your assets. Take the uncertainty out of this process. Write down who you would want to have your automobile. Write down what you want done with the family home. They can't all live in it. Write down which items of your jewelry you want them to have. They will probably all want your favorite pieces of jewelry.

You can purchase a will kit at a nominal fee. I, of course, suggest you see an attorney. Based on your financial situation, you may need estate planning advice. Sometimes it is better to convey items while you are alive opposed to letting them flow through the will.

I once probated a family's will. In that case, the father transferred ownership of his high ticket items while he was still alive, but retained a life estate interest which allowed him to use the property until his death. The property was distributed outside the will immediately to his beneficiaries.

Most wills provide that all debts be paid. I would advise that life insurance proceeds not be distributed through the will, because you want to protect the money from creditors. Probating a will can take up to a year or so, but your family may need the money right away. My personal preference is to get my inheritance while my parents are alive. If I can't get it, please make a will and put it in a safe place. Let a trusted family member know where your will is kept. This will prevent relatives from fighting over items. Every one will know how you want your property distributed. You have exercised power over your assets.

Joan is an only child. Both of her parents passed away within a period of several years. Her mother had money in the retirement system and had her brother as the beneficiary. Prior to her death, she requested the paperwork to change beneficiary to her daughter. Before she could mail it back in, she died. Who do you think is legally entitled to the proceeds? The brother, of course, is entitled to them. Who do you think she wanted to inherit her money? Obviously, she wanted her daughter to take possession of her assets.

Now, we have a dilemma. Do you think her brother was willing to relinquish the funds. Oh, but no. And now, we had a grieving child who had to deal with this unfortunate situation. Her mother had medical expenses and bills that needed to be paid, but the daughter could not pay them until she received the money. Joan had to hire an attorney to get the matter taken care of. But, this situation could have been avoided. A grieving person does not need such unnecessary financial matters to deal with.

A lot of people get separated from their spouse, but never get around to getting a divorce. For example, I had a recently widowed woman come into my office. She had been separated from her husband, for ten years but never got around to getting a divorce. She wanted to know what she needed to do to get her husband's property from his mistress. I told her that legally she was his heir. A week later, she drove to his rental house where his mistress still lived. She had a wrecker tow away all of his automobiles plus she took the furniture and his clothes. I am sure that he probably wanted his mistress to have all these things, but he he'd left no will. He knew that he was still married but instead of taking control of his property, he let the government disburse it for him.

Beth came into my office one day needing advice on her rights to the family home. Her mother had recently died of a long illness. She lived with her and had been her primary caretaker. Her four siblings lived out of state. They rarely came home to check on their mother. She told me that her mother had said on numerous occasions that she wanted the house and its contents to go to Beth, yet, she did not make a will. Her siblings came home for the funeral and immediately began staking claim to household items and talked of selling the house and splitting the proceeds.

Beth told them, "Mom wanted me to have the house. I took care of her; none of you did a thing." Was Beth entitled to the house? Morally, she may have been, but if her mother wanted to disinherit her other children, then she needed to have taken steps to do so while she was alive. Legally, all five of the ckildren were the mother's heirs. They all had an equal interest in the property.

On one occasion, I had a family come into my office in shambles. Their aunt had recently died. She had no husband or children and had left ten thousand dollars in the bank, with no beneficiary designated. She had no will. The family needed the money for her funeral. We had to file papers to get the money released and would take weeks to get the money. Black people are known for taking a long time to bury a loved one, but this wait was out of the question. That family had to borrow money to bury their aunt. Again, this problem could have been eliminated had she left a beneficiary on her account or had the money distributed through her will.

Five Year Estate Checklist

Have you updated your will in the last five years?

Does your life insurance beneficiary need to be updated?

Does your pension plan have a designated beneficiary?

Do all of your bank accounts have a designated beneficiary?

Do you have beneficiaries on your stocks?

SECTION FIVE
THE PERSONAL

Chapter Sixteen

If You Don't Take Care of Yourself, Who Will Care for Your Children

> *It's all about priorities, and my priority now is being a Mom. I am happy and so fulfilled that I have never felt I've had more purpose in my life than right now.*
> —Jada Pinkett Smith

Sunday dinner in the movie "Soul Food", reminded me of so many times we had during the holidays in the Johnson household. Our lives revolved around food. The aroma of chitterlings, turnip greens, macaroni and cheese, turkey and dressing, ham, and apple cobbler greeted you at the door. Although we love these foods, you have to realize there is a direct correlation between eating habits and diseases such as diabetes, high blood pressure, cancer and strokes. Health care is one of the most critical issues facing women. More women are overweight, leading to hypertension, heart disease, diabetes, and strokes. If we are not healthy, who will take care of our children?

As wives, mothers, and lovers sometimes we have to be selfish with our time. I know women who get so caught up in the lives of their mate and children that they forget to take care of themselves. They put off that yearly pap smear.

The scale continues to climb and with it, so do the weight related diseases. It is imperative that we take time out of our busy schedules to do a breast self-examination. It can be done in a matter of seconds while you are in the shower.

In April of 1999, after I had my son, Trey, his pediatrician came to talk to me. I was on the phone with my secretary trying to take care of some business. He interrupted the conversation to tell me, "Mom, you need to slow down. You will be better able to take care of your son, if you first take care of yourself." How dare he tell me what to do," I proceeded to tell him, "Are you here to lecture me or to talk to me about Trey?" Instead of lecturing him, I should have heeded his warning.

I brought the new millennium in with a bang. I closed a law practice and started a new job; My husband's job transferred him to another state; My son was eight months old, and I was four months pregnant with my second child. My body was telling me to slow down. But, my mind shouted back, "You're a strong woman; You can handle anything!." We cannot be all things to all people. Like a rubber band, we can stretch only so far until the elastic eventually breaks.

In March of 2000, I flew to San Fransico to attend a conference. Three of my girlfriends were going to meet me there, too. It felt like de ja vu. As a girl, I had traveled to San Fransico vicariously by reading various Danielle Steele novels, but now it was real! My girlfriends and I toured San Fransico, saw the sites and shopped until we dropped. On our last night, we had dinner at a local comedy club. The star attraction was Robin Williams and I thought we were about to see a celebrity impersonator, but no, the Robin Williams, you know, the one from Mrs. Doubtfire, walked on the stage. We couldn't believe it! We started jumping and high fiving each other. He was hilarious! We were one of just a few black people in the club. Mr. Williams made a comment, "Look at those lovely sisters sitting at that table." We thought he was so correct. We were looking good!

When I came home from my trip, I discovered my two year old Siberian Husky, Max, had gotten out of the yard while I was away. I called the next day to say I was coming to get him. They told me that he had broken out of the pound. Yeah, right! My dog was not Houdini! By then, I was very pissed off. In my mind, "I knew that they gave my dog to someone." When they showed me the cage my dog had been in, another dog was already in it. So, if my dog had really broken out of it, why was another dog already in the same cage?

As if I weren't stressed out enough, a week after my trip while at home, I started to have abdominal pains followed by vaginal bleeding. I drove myself to the hospital and after an exam was informed that I was in labor I was fully dilated, so the doctor gave me medicine to prolong the labor. I was informed that the baby was coming, it was a matter of when. I was given steroids to help the baby's lungs develop. I thought to myself, "How could this be happening?" I am only twenty-four weeks into my pregnancy.

Three days later, I gave birth to a one pound twelve ounce baby boy. After seeing Miles, no matter what anyone said, I felt like I had done something wrong. What if I had slown down, maybe things would be different. Two days after Miles was born, the neonatologist came to my room and informed us that he suspected that Miles had a cranial bleed. They were doing x-rays to confirm it. I started to cry, surely this was my curse for not listening, but thank God, he returned an hour later and said that the x-rays were negative. Miles stayed in the hospital for four months. He was released in July. So far he is doing okay.

Two weeks before Christmas, my dog, Max, showed up at my doorstep, nine months after he had disappeared. He looked like he had been to hell and back. I hardly recognized him. My husband said, "Max is home. It's going to be a good Christmas." That it was. But, Max lived for only another month before he died. In 2000, I learned that faith in God, family, and friends are the most important things in life. They give you the power to put one foot in front of the other and keep moving when all you want to do, otherwise, is quit.

Chapter Seventeen

Health Issues Facing Women

In the early 1990's, I read a report that predicted by the year 2000 that every American would have a relative or know someone who had AIDS. I did not take that report very seriously. It did not apply to me or anyone I knew. After all, we were normal and this was a disease of drug addicts and sexual deviants.

But in 1995, I learned that my grandmother had full blown AIDS. You would never expect a grandparent to contract such a dreaded, sexually transmitted disease. But she like other women contracted this disease from their supposedly heterosexual partners.

In a short span of three months, we watched as my grandmother's health deteriorated. In September, she was up and walking, but by November, she was confined to a wheelchair. In December, she died. I will never forget the last words she spoke to me, " You know that I am dying." It tore me to pieces to see such a lovely lady die so young. The sad thing is could have been prevented. I vowed that I would take precautions and not become another AIDS statistic.

In 1996, as a child support attorney with the Department of Human Services, I saw that women were not taking AIDS seriously. By not taking it seriously, they were playing Russian Roulette with their lives. Young women would come into our office with one child on the hip and two toddlers lagging behind them. The children would be by three different men. They were having sex with virtual strangers. I wanted to scream and tell them, "Don't you know that AIDS kills!"

Symptoms of AIDS

HIV/Aids has a number of symptoms but it may take many years before those symptoms surface. They include:

1. Persistent Fatigue

2. Unexplained Fever

3. Drenching night sweats

4. Unexplained weight loss

5. Swollen glands

6. Persistent diarrhea

7. Dry cough

AIDS Preventive Measures:

Here is how you can greatly reduce the risk of contracting AIDS:

1) Maintain monogamous relationship with a HIV negative partner.

2) Use condoms.

3) Do not share needles

4) Reduce risky sexual behavior.

It's Okay to Seek Help

As a child, I remember this or that cousin bunking in my room while their parents tried to "work it out." Grown folks would discuss the couple's problem. Occasionally, we would hear someone ask, "Are they going to counseling?" They would reply, "You know most people don't do the 'counseling thing'. This always struck me as odd and it strikes even closer to home now. We need to realize that it is okay to seek help when you need it. It is okay to question the validity of your existence. It is okay not to know who you are. Have the common sense to seek professional help so you can find yourself.

You don't always have to be the strong one and you won't always have all the answers. Sometimes, you will get depressed and distressed. When you break a bone, you go see an orthopedic doctor. When you get pregnant, you go see an obstetrician. Ladies, when you are stressed and questioning your existence and can't seem to cope, you need to see a psychiatrist. When your marriage is sick, you need to see a Marriage or Family Therapist, or better yet, your Pastor!

Your mental health is just as important, if not more important, than your physical health. For when the brain dies, you cease to function. If we are not mentally healthy, how do we expect our children to be? If we don't ask and seek help, how can we be sure that they will if they need help? The time of the therapist's couch being "taboo" is gone. The time of taking care of yourself mentally is now.

Chapter Eighteen

Set Aside Me Time

My house is going to have a lot of Mirrors, because, I love to get my daily dose of me.
—Serena Williams

Women are waking up to find out that life is passing us by. As we stare into the mirror, we see yesterday's hairdo, a face with no make-up and a broken spirit. How do we reclaim our identity? How do we find out what truly makes us happy?

After having two children in less than a two year span, I was in an internal funk. I felt fat and unattractive. In my mind, I had to do something drastic to make myself feel better. I went to the beauty shop and told my beautician to cut it all off. I had worn a chin length bob for the past three years and watched as my beautiful black locks were cut and fell to the floor. I remember thinking to myself, "My husband is going to kill me!"

But it was a magical transformation. Instantly, I felt taller and thinner. My face suddenly had a new glow. I received "cat" calls that I hadn't received in years. A haircut may not be what it takes to lift your spirits, but it can be a good start. Go out and buy yourself a new outfit. Get a makeover at the mall. Whatever it takes, do something to make yourself feel sexy.

Leave the children at home with your husband or get a babysitter. Call your girlfriends up and have a girls' night out. Being with a group of ladies is calming. Problems have a way of working themselves out. No matter what kind of stress we face—whether it's a funky job, a failing marriage or those bad children, the company of other ladies can help us to get through it. Our conversations are not about solutions. They are about comfort and consolation. My friends and I get together and go out for drinks. We laugh about our jobs, our husbands, and our children. It is so refreshing and after our date is over, I am ready to face another day.

Beauty/Relaxation Secrets

*Meditation

Your spiritual and mental health is just as important as your physical health. You have to take time out to talk to whatever higher power you believe in. This does not have to take place inside a church, chapel, or synagogue. I talk to God as I drive to work in the morning. First, I go over the previous day with myself. I talk about what I did right or wrong and what I need to do better. I talk about who got on my last nerve, or who was just too sweet. After I complete this process with myself, I turn it over to God, my Higher Power. If I messed up, I ask Him to help me do better. If I went slam off, I ask Him to grant me more patience. If I did an outstanding job, I thank Him for his guidance and help. This entire process takes fifteen minutes. I know we all have fifteen minutes to spare in a given day to get ourselves mentally and spiritually prepared for the day to come. Try it. This will do wonders for your attitude and your peace of mind.

The Personal

*Bubble Bath

There are few things as relaxing as a bubble bath. Take one! Let your shower fill your tub. This will create steam and moisture. It gives you the spa atmosphere without the spa price. Place candles around the tub or sink area. You can purchase aroma therapy candles for less than two dollars each. Now, turn off the overhead lights. Place a folded towel over the back of the tub to pillow your head. If you live alone, get in. If you don't live alone, place a sign that reads, "Do not disturb for the next thirty minutes" or years (whatever you like) on the door. Now, step into that tub.

For the next thirty minutes, focus on you. Tell yourself how good you are looking and feeling. Compliment yourself on the good job you are doing at work. Praise yourself for refraining from having that cheesecake at lunch. The point is during that thirty minutes, the most important person in the world is you. Concentrate on your relaxation and enjoyment. So, let it be written. So, let it be done.

*Massage

You always hear women talking about getting their hair, nails, or toes done. When was the last time you heard anyone talking about getting her body done, by a massage therapist that is? The answer to that question is rare to never, unless you are friends with the likes of Halle Berry, Cindy Crawford, Janet Jackson, or Oprah Winfrey.

I am very fortunate; my husband is a licensed massage therapist. Ladies, there is nothing more relaxing than having the strong hands of a man rub and knead all of your tension, knots, and stress away. It is therapeutic and relatively inexpensive ($30-40) for a professional.

However, you may have an undercover massage therapist in your own home. I suggest you ask him. Until you ask, you will never know. If he says he doesn't know how, check out a friendly bookstore. You'll find it has books on the proper techniques. Go out and buy a copy. Learn how to massage him, then encourage him to master the technique, so he can return the favor. It'll work wonders for both of you - and your relationship.

*Light the Candles and Pop the Cork
Put the kids to bed early. Take out the bubble bath. Put on your favorite negligee. Soften the lights and light the candles. Put on your favorite Brian McKnight melody and pop the cork on your favorite wine. Dance slowly and seductively with your mate. Let your mind travel back to the beginning of your relationship when everything was fresh and new. Take your time and undress each other. Make this a very special night for you and your man.

Chapter Nineteen

I Am Responsible For My Own Happiness

It's my life and I have to take responsibility for it. Over the past three years, I've been broke, dumped and pimped. I learned I had to believe in myself and not just to be comfortable with the opinions of others. I'm just more in control. I dot the I's and cross the T's. Like Scarlett O'Hara, I won't be broke again......
—Toni Braxton, 2000

How many of us like ourselves just the way we are? If the answer is "I do", great! However, if the answer is "I don't", then ask yourself, why not? What can you do about it? I will tell you, change. To me, change equals growth. You don't stop growing until you die. Now, I don't mean physical growth, although some of us do continue to grow out. I mean mentally. But I'm talking about mental and spiritual growth. Why do you think Christopher Reeves (Superman) who is now paralyzed can still direct movies, It's because he's using his mental power. Why do you think Teddy Pendergrass continues to perform sold out concerts? It's because he has harnessed his mental power.

If you don't like who you are, harness your mental power and change. No matter what your physical circumstance, your mind can be your key to freedom and growth. Take a class, there are some offered for free at your local junior college. Also, check your public library for "How To" books and make it an adventure by learning on your own.

Who is a positive influence in your life? Why are they? You should make them your mentors. Don't be afraid to pick their brains. Ask them how did they achieve the things in life they did? You may be surprised that they share a similar background with you. Who do you know that has what you want? Who has a more lively personality? Who has a more straightforward way of doing things?

Ask them how they got there. Take notes and post them up on your bathroom mirror. If you don't want to ask them, observe what they do and write it down. If they have a plan for success, copy it. Don't reinvent the wheel. The end result should be that it makes you happy in who you are. It makes you comfortable to be in your skin. It puts you on the path to gaining the power.

Who am I? What do I want from life? How am I going to achieve it? How long is it going to take me to achieve it? Do I need help achieving it? Is there anyone who can help me achieve it? Does this person value me enough to help me achieve it? Is it realistic? Can I achieve it? What am I waiting on? Power is strength over time. The only power someone has over you is the power you give them.

Ladies, if no one has ever told you how magnificent you are, I am telling you now. If no one has ever told you how intelligent you are, I am telling you now. If no one has ever told you that you can be anything, do anything, go anywhere, I am telling you now. If no one has ever told you that you are a success, I am telling you now. If no one has ever told you that you can do it, I am telling you now. If no one has ever told you that you are somebody, I am telling you now. If no one has ever told you that you have the power, I am telling you now. You have the Power. As my grandfather used to say, we gave you the keys to the car, and it's all powered up. It is now up to you to get in the car—and drive!

Understand Your Role in Your Marriage

I have heard women say, "He's a dawg. Then she'll go on to say that he did this, that and the other to me." We all have found ourselves in unhealthy relationships. But before anyone else can make you happy, you need to know what makes you happy. You have to have inner love and strength for yourself. At the end of the day, when all is said and done, you're responsible for your own happiness. Pick up the pieces and move on. You have the power to control your destiny.

When I first got married, my entire life revolved around my husband. I wanted to be with him all the time. My mission in life was to please him. If he wanted to go to the movies, whether I wanted to go or not, I would say yes. He would say, "Well, what do you want to see?" I would reply, "Whatever you want to see." He said, "It's not about what I want. You cannot compromise your happiness for me. You have to do what makes you happy." One day he pulled me aside and said, "I need my space." I realized I had lost myself in him. He had friends. I needed to go out and find a life for myself. Women often attach happiness to a man, but you need your own identity. Your mate cannot be your sole source of happiness. You will smother him to death if you don't give him some space.

Your mate is not responsible for your happiness, nor is he responsible for your unhappiness. You and only you must take responsibility for that. Your childhood is not the cause of your adult unhappiness. If you have not conquered that child in the mirror, it is time for you to replace that child with a new and improved woman. Your race or sex is not an excuse for your being unhappy or depressed. Accept your lot in life and learn to live with it. Power is strength over time.

More importantly, you need to understand your respective roles in your marriage. Put God as the head of your life. Next, believe that God made man in his own image and placed him as head of the family. God-fashioned woman out of man. He wants us to support our husbands. God commanded man to honor and love his wife, placing her before all others. When we remember this, we stand united and our bond is stronger. When this is forgotten, the relationship becomes unstable and our bond is fragile.

Over the years, my husband and I have both inflicted pain on each other. We have made mistakes and choices that were not always right. The wonderful thing is that we are blessed to recognize and accept our faults. We work diligently towards keeping "us" together. I don't advocate staying in an abusive relationship. There are some people who should have never been together in the first place. Nonetheless, for those couples, who truly love one another and are equally committed to maintaining a stable, loving relationship, the journey is worth any sacrifices made.

If you are single and are looking to marry, make sure you are marrying someone who adds to your life. You don't need someone who complicates life. If you are already in a relationship or marriage, you and your partner need to share similar values, goals and dreams. If not, the things that brought you together will never be enough to maintain the relationship. The dynamics of the relationship may change with the introduction of children, new jobs, and financial problems. But your fundamental values will always remain true. Your marriage will have staying power. *Your Family Will Have The Power!*

Afterword

This venture between Vanessa and I did not start out as a book. Actually it started out as a dream to tour the country talking to other women. We saw how lucrative it was for personnel in the profession. Being that neither of us is shy and we could make money by talking to people, we, thought, why not? We could do what we loved and make lots of money in the process what a bargain!

We came up with a topic. We were off and running. However as we began to write, we noticed that the shared pasts and issues were ones that could touch the lives of others and help them grow and become better. Money no longer was the driving factor, but the need to help other women on the journey called success.

So we say thank you to all of you, the young, middle aged, and forever young who will read this book. You have become our inspiration and the catharsis to deal with issues that we all have to overcome. You helped us to see that life is bigger than just us, and that we all intertwined in a sisterhood that is universal and bigger than race, religion, creed, or color. You gave us a purpose for sharing our gift. We pray that you enjoyed this work, and the works to come. Pray for us as we will for you. For although we now have the power, He is All Powerful (can I get an Amen!).

Notes

Chapter Two

Woodson, C.G. (1993). *The Mis-Education of the Negro*. 6th ed. Trenton, NJ: Africa World Press.

Chapter Five

Williams, T. and Cooney, J. (1994). *The Personal Touch*. New York, NY: Warner Books, Inc.

Woodson, C. G. (1993). *The Mis-Education of the Negro*. 6th ed. Trenton, NJ: Africa World Press.

Chapter Twelve

Hopson, D. S. and Hopson D. P. (1995). *Friends and Lovers*. New York, NY: Fireside.

Wade, B. and Richardson, B (1993). *Love Lessons*. New York, NY: Amistad Press.

Chapter Fourteen

McAleese, T. (1993). *Get Rich Slow*. 2nd ed. Hawthorne, N.J.: The Career Press.

Chapter Fifteen

McAleese, T (1993). *Get Rich Slow*. 2nd ed. Hawthorne, N.J.: The Career Press.

Chapter Sixteen

McAleese, T. (1993). *Get Rich Slow*. 2nd ed. Hawthorne, N.J.: The Career Press.

Index

abuse,
    in childhood, 0, 6
    in relationships, 131
    Physical, 9, 19, 123, 126, 129-130
acne, 4, 6
acting white, 11
adoration, 64
affairs, see infidelity
after college, 58
AIDS
    Symptoms, 122
    Preventive measures, 122
Angelou, Maya, 9
anger, 66, 72, 74, 86
appointment, 22, 28, 39
asset, 65
attitude, 28, 31, 38, 40-43, 46, 48, 51, 126
Automobile, 96, 107, 110

baggage, 76
beneficiary, 111-113
Berry, Halle, 127
booty call, 67, 77
Braxton, Toni, 129
breast cancer, 70
broke, 23, 65, 67, 95, 105-106, 108, 129
bubble bath, 127-128
business, 0, 21, 31, 44, 52, 60, 73, 81, 95, 102, 105, 118

candles, 91, 127-128
career, see work, workplace
characteristics, 58, 74
childhood
    Attitudes toward family formed in, 33
    Role models in, 13, 45-46
    Self-esteem, 4, 14, 37
child support, 45, 67, 74, 121
civil rights, 20
commitment, 87, 98

communication, 72, 84
compassion, 31, 58
compromise, 0, 69-70, 131
confidence, 0, 4, 14, 17, 23
conflict, 31, 84
Cosign, 68
Crawford, Cindy, 127
credit card, 99
credit rating, 68
cut losses, 36

dating, 71, 73, 81, 107
Dutch, 58
daycare, 86, 89
discrimination, in workplace, 31
divorce, 72, 76, 83, 111
drama, 0, 60, 66
dating, 71, 73, 81, 107
Dutch, 58

education, differences in
    Child, 0, 3-5, 7, 9, 13-14, 45, 47, 60, 67, 73-74, 86, 103, 107, 111, 118, 121, 123, 132
ego, 0, 89
employment, see work, workplace
estate checklist, 113
estate planning, 110

faith, 51, 87, 120
families
    Dysfunctional, 12
fiancé, 58-59
finances
    Setting priorities, 24, 73, 117
friends, 0, 10, 12, 18, 23, 28, 33, 38, 59, 66, 69-71, 80, 83, 102-103, 120, 126-127, 131, 135

girls' night out, 126
goals, 0, 17, 31-34, 71, 73, 75, 133
God, 0, 6, 12, 20-21, 29, 57-58, 60-61, 95, 120, 126, 132

health issues, 0, 121
    Hypertension, 117
    Heart disease, 117
    Diabetes, 117
    Strokes, 97, 117
    Weight, 4-5, 118, 122
    Pap smear, 117
hoodlums, 60
household
    Communication, 72, 84
    Self-esteem, 4, 14, 37

insurance
    Term life, 105-106
    Whole life, 105-106
    Automobile, 96, 107, 110
    Uninsured motorist, 107
    Liability, 45, 65, 107
interview, 30, 39, 41-43, 54

Jackson, Janet, 127
job, see workplace
Johnston Island, 60

Kiss, 64, 75, 89, 91

law school, 24
liability, 45, 65, 107
love, 0-1, 3-5, 7, 14, 32, 45, 53-54, 57, 59-60, 63-64, 70, 74-75, 77, 79-80, 82, 85, 87, 90-91, 117, 125, 131-132, 135

Marriage
    Divorce and, 76
Massage, 64, 127-128
Meditation, 126
Men
    Control and, 11
    Characteristics sought in, 58, 74
    Violent, 32, 66
Money, see finances
mother-in-law, 67, 79-80
Mother Theresa, 85

obsession, 59
office
   Dress, 43, 51-52
   Hair, 4-5, 36, 40, 44, 49, 51-52, 65, 96, 99, 127
   Make-up, 49, 52, 125
   Shoes, 43, 52, 76, 85, 98
   Jewelry, 52, 110
   Perfume, 52
   Nails, 52-53, 65, 96, 99, 127
opinion, 5, 51
ostracize, 51

Pendergrass, Teddy, 129
portfolio, 0, 49, 78
prince charming, 58

racism, 28, 44
recycling, 9
Reeves, Christopher, 129
Relationships
   Clarifying goals in, 17, 31-34, 71, 73, 75, 133
   Common mistakes in, 14 ,96, 132
   Sex in balance of, 4, 31, 67-68, 73-75, 90-91, 122, 132
   Warning signals, 74
Religion, 139
respect, 0, 10, 45, 71, 77, 80, 87
retirement, 95-97, 111
Role models, 13, 45-46

sacrifice, 23, 63, 96
saint, 58-59
savior, 59
self-esteem
   Impact of role models*, 13, 45-46
   Making peace with past and, 76, 100, 129
soul food, 117
Steele, Danielle, 13, 118
success, 6, 10, 13-14, 23-24, 38, 43-45, 51, 130-131, 139

terminator, 59
toilet, 70-72

Uncle Sam, 28, 95
understanding, 59-61, 73

Waiting to Exhale, 58
water, 9, 67, 71, 87
wedding, 5, 78-79
welfare, 45
Williams, Robin, 118
Williams, Serena, 125
Williams, Terrie, 44-45
Winfrey, Oprah, 31, 127
Woodson, Carter G., 32
work ethic, 34
work, job
    Experience, 12, 19, 28, 41, 44, 46